# THE TEENAGER WHISPERER

## NAVIGATING ADOLESCENCE WITH GRACE

DR. MINAKSHI BANSAL

# DEDICATION

*This book is dedicated to the teenagers who are bravely navigating the complex journey of adolescence. Your resilience, curiosity, and capacity for growth inspire me every day. May you find the strength and wisdom to embrace your true selves, and may this book offer you the guidance and support you need along the way.*

*To the parents, caregivers, and mentors who tirelessly support these young individuals, your dedication, empathy, and unwavering love create the foundation upon which they build their futures. Your commitment to guiding them with patience and understanding is invaluable.*

*To my own mentors and guides, whose wisdom and compassion have shaped my path, thank you for your enduring support and for showing me the power of empathy and connection.*

*And finally, to my family, for their endless encouragement and belief in my work. Your love and support have made this book possible. Thank you for being my constant source of strength and inspiration.*

ᚦᚦᚦ

# Contents

# Contents

# Prayer

*"Om Bhadram Karnebhih Shrinuyama Devah*

*Bhadram Pashyemakshabhiryajatrah*

*Sthirairangais Tushtuvamsastanubhih*

*Vyashema Devahitam Yadayuh*

*Svasti Na Indro Vriddhashravah*

*Svasti Nah Pusha Vishwavedah*

*Svasti Nastarkshyo Arishtanemih*

*Svasti No Brihaspatir Dadhatu*

*Om Shantih Shantih Shantih"*

*This mantra is a prayer for universal well-being, invoking the blessings of various deities for protection, health, and happiness. It emphasizes the importance of experiencing the auspicious through all senses and living a life aligned with divine purpose. The repetition of "Shantih" at the end signifies a deep desire for peace in the individual, the environment, and the universe at large. This mantra is often recited as a prayer for peace, prosperity, and the physical and spiritual well-being of all beings.*

ppp

# About The Author

This book represents the culmination of extensive research and meticulous analysis, incorporating a diverse range of sources, including numerous books, scholarly studies, and personal experiences. Additionally, I have scoured various websites to gather relevant information and data essential for the compilation of this work. I have taken every precaution to ensure the accuracy of the information presented and have diligently cited all sources to acknowledge their contributions.

From her earliest days, Minakshi was distinguished by an insatiable appetite for reading. Her literary universe was inhabited by characters and narratives that spanned ethical tales, motivational and inspirational stories, and the mythic parables imbued with life lessons. This voracious reading habit was not merely for personal edification but was driven by a desire to distill and disseminate the essence of these narratives to foster the development of students and peers alike. She was particularly captivated by the lives and teachings of historical figures and spiritual leaders such as Adi Shankaracharya, Swami Vivekananda, Dr. APJ Abdul Kalam, Mahamana Pandit Madan Mohan Malviya, Mahatma Gandhi, Sardar Vallabhai Patel, and Vinoba Bhave, among others. Their philosophies and life stories fueled her ambition to embody their ideals of resilience, selflessness, and relentless pursuit of knowledge.

Dr. Minakshi's academic and practical engagement with psychology has been equally noteworthy. As a research scholar, her focus has been on exploring the intricate tapestry of the human psyche, aiming to unlock the potential for psychological well-being and societal harmony. Her scholarly work is complemented by her active involvement in social work, where she employs her academic insights to make tangible differences in the lives of the underprivileged. Her endeavours in social work are characterized by an innovative approach that combines traditional wisdom with contemporary psychological practices to address the multifaceted challenges faced by these communities.

Her artistic talents, another facet of her diverse capabilities, are not merely a personal passion but also serve as a medium through which she communicates and connects with others. Her art, rich in symbolism and emotional depth, reflects her philosophical inquiries and social concerns, offering viewers a glimpse into the breadth of her intellect and the depth of her compassion.

In addition to her contributions to the arts and social sciences, Dr. Minakshi has embraced the healing arts of Pranic Healing, mastering the techniques developed by Master Choa Kok Sui. This practice, which focuses on the manipulation of Prana or life energy to heal the body and aura, has been both a personal journey of discovery and a means through which she extends her healing touch to others. Her proficiency in Pranic Healing is complemented by her advocacy and teaching of various forms of meditation aimed at rejuvenation, personal betterment, and the cultivation of harmony within individuals and communities alike.

Dr. Minakshi's life is a narrative of relentless pursuit, not just of personal achievement but of the upliftment and empowerment of society at large. Her diverse interests and talents—spanning the arts, literature, psychology, and the healing practices—converge on a singular path of service. She embodies the spirit of the luminaries who inspired her, channelling their legacy through her actions and teachings. Through her books, art, and social initiatives, she continues to inspire a new generation to embark on their own journeys of self-discovery, resilience, and altruism.

Her commitment to social betterment, particularly her focus on uplifting underprivileged children, reflects a deep understanding of the transformative potential of education and personal development. By integrating her knowledge of psychology, her artistic sensibilities, and her healing practices, Dr. Bansal has developed a holistic approach to social work that addresses both the immediate needs and the long-term well-being of the communities she serves.

As an author, Dr. Minakshi's writings offer a blend of inspirational insights, practical wisdom, and reflective contemplations drawn from her extensive reading and life experiences. Her books serve as a guide for those seeking to navigate the complexities of life with grace, resilience, and purpose. Through her narratives, she extends an invitation to her readers to explore the depths of their own potential and to contribute meaningfully to the collective well-being of society.

In Dr. Minakshi Bansal, we find a remarkable synthesis of the artist, the scholar, the healer, and the social activist. Her life's work stands as a beacon of hope and a source of inspiration for individuals seeking to make a difference in the world. Her story is a compelling reminder of the power of individual action, rooted in compassion and driven by a profound commitment to the betterment of humanity. Dr. Minakshi's legacy is not just in the tangible outcomes of her efforts but in the enduring spirit of inquiry, empathy, and service that she embodies.

ppp

# Preface

As I embarked on the journey of writing this book, I was driven by a profound desire to connect with teenagers and the adults who care for them. Adolescence is a unique and transformative period, filled with both challenges and opportunities. It is a time when young people are forging their identities, testing boundaries, and navigating a complex world. My hope is to offer insights and guidance that can help teenagers and their families traverse this critical stage with understanding, empathy, and grace.

Growing up, I was fortunate to have mentors who understood the intricacies of adolescence. Their wisdom and support were invaluable, shaping my path and helping me become the person I am today. As I reflect on those formative years, I realize how essential it is for teenagers to have someone who listens, understands, and guides them without judgment. This book is an extension of that realization, a tribute to the mentors and caregivers who play such a pivotal role in young lives.

Throughout my career, I have had the privilege of working with teenagers in various capacities. Each interaction has deepened my understanding of their struggles, dreams, and potential. Teenagers today face a rapidly changing world, where the pressures of social media, academic expectations, and global uncertainties can be overwhelming. Yet, despite these challenges, they possess an incredible resilience and capacity for growth. My goal is to highlight this resilience and provide strategies that can help teenagers thrive.

One of the most important lessons I have learned is the power of empathy. Adolescence can be a tumultuous time, and it is easy for adults to forget what it felt like to navigate those years. Empathy allows us to step into the shoes of teenagers, to see the world through their eyes, and to understand their experiences. This understanding is the foundation of effective communication and support. By fostering empathy, we can build stronger, more trusting relationships with teenagers, guiding them through their challenges and celebrating their successes.

Communication is another cornerstone of navigating adolescence. Teenagers need to feel heard and valued, and open, honest communication is essential for building trust. This involves not only listening to their words but also understanding the emotions behind them. It means creating a safe space where they can express themselves without fear of criticism or rejection. Through effective communication, we can address misunderstandings, resolve conflicts, and support teenagers in making informed decisions.

Encouraging independence and responsibility is crucial during the teenage years. As young people grow, they need opportunities to make choices, take risks, and learn from their experiences. This process helps them develop a sense of autonomy and prepares them for adulthood. It is important to strike a balance between providing guidance and allowing them the freedom to explore. By empowering teenagers to take ownership of their actions, we help them build confidence and resilience.

Understanding the adolescent mind is key to supporting teenagers effectively. The teenage brain is still developing, particularly in areas related to decision-making, impulse control, and emotional regulation. This biological reality can explain some of the behaviors and challenges associated with adolescence. By acknowledging the developmental stage teenagers are in, we can approach their actions with greater patience and understanding. It also underscores the importance of providing clear boundaries and consistent support as they navigate this critical period.

Healthy relationships are fundamental to a teenager's well-being. This includes relationships with family, friends, teachers, and mentors. Positive relationships provide a sense of belonging, support, and security. They help teenagers develop social skills, empathy, and a sense of community. It is important to model healthy relationships and teach teenagers how to build and maintain them. This involves fostering respect, trust, communication, and conflict resolution skills. By nurturing these relationships, we can help teenagers develop a strong social network that supports their growth and well-being.

The role of technology in teenagers' lives cannot be overlooked. While technology offers many benefits, it also presents challenges such as cyberbullying, social comparison, and digital addiction. Helping teenagers navigate the digital world responsibly is essential. This involves setting boundaries around technology use, encouraging critical thinking about online content, and promoting healthy online behavior. It also means being aware of the impact of social media on self-esteem and mental health and providing support as they navigate these challenges.

Mental health is a critical aspect of adolescence. Teenagers are at a higher risk for mental health issues such as anxiety, depression, and stress. It is essential to create an environment where mental health is prioritized and stigmas are reduced. This involves recognizing the signs of mental health issues, providing access to resources, and encouraging open conversations about mental health. By supporting teenagers' mental health, we can help them build resilience and coping skills that will serve them throughout their lives.

Encouraging creativity and self-expression is another important aspect of supporting teenagers. Creative activities provide an outlet for emotions, foster a sense of accomplishment, and enhance problem-solving skills. Whether through art, music, writing, or other forms of expression, creativity allows teenagers to explore their identities and connect with others. Providing opportunities for creative expression can help teenagers develop confidence and a sense of purpose.

Physical health is equally important during the teenage years. Encouraging healthy lifestyle choices, such as regular exercise, balanced nutrition, and adequate sleep, supports overall well-being. Physical activity can reduce stress, improve mood, and enhance cognitive function. Educating teenagers about the importance of self-care and healthy habits can help them make informed choices that benefit their physical and mental health.

As teenagers prepare for the future, it is important to provide guidance and support in their academic and career planning. This involves helping them set realistic goals, explore their interests, and develop the skills needed for success. Providing opportunities for career exploration, such as internships, job shadowing, and mentorship, can help them make informed decisions about their future paths. Encouraging a growth mindset, where effort and persistence are valued, can also help teenagers develop resilience and a love of learning.

Coping with failure and setbacks is a crucial life skill. Teenagers need to learn that failure is a natural part of life and an opportunity for growth. Encouraging them to view setbacks as learning experiences, rather than as reflections of their worth, can help them build resilience and perseverance. Providing support and guidance during difficult times, and celebrating their efforts and progress, can help them develop a positive and proactive approach to challenges.

Empathy and volunteerism are also important aspects of personal growth. Encouraging teenagers to volunteer and give back to their communities fosters a sense of responsibility and compassion. Volunteering provides valuable life experiences, teaches important skills, and helps teenagers develop empathy and social awareness.

It also provides a sense of purpose and fulfillment, contributing to their overall well-being.

Creating a safe and supportive home environment is the foundation of all these efforts. A nurturing home provides the stability and security teenagers need to thrive. This involves being present, showing unconditional love and support, and creating an environment where they feel valued and understood. It also means setting clear boundaries, providing guidance, and allowing them the freedom to grow and explore. By creating a safe and supportive home, we can help teenagers navigate the challenges of adolescence and develop into confident, resilient, and compassionate adults.

In writing this book, I have drawn upon my own experiences, both personal and professional, as well as extensive research and insights from experts in the field. My aim is to provide practical advice, thoughtful reflections, and compassionate guidance for navigating the teenage years. I hope to offer a roadmap for parents, caregivers, educators, and teenagers themselves, to help them navigate this critical period with grace and understanding.

*Dr. Minakshi Bansal*
*Social Activist*
*Ahmedabad, Gujarat, Bharat*

# ONE

## UNDERSTANDING THE ADOLESCENT MIND

Understanding the adolescent mind requires a deep dive into the complex and rapidly changing world of teenagers. Adolescence is a period of significant growth and development, marked by profound physical, emotional, cognitive, and social changes. These changes are driven by a combination of biological processes, psychological developments, and environmental influences.

Biologically, adolescence is characterized by puberty, a time when the body undergoes dramatic transformations. Hormonal changes trigger the development of secondary sexual characteristics, such as breast development in girls and increased muscle mass in boys. These physical changes can significantly impact a teenager's self-esteem and body image. The surge in hormones, particularly testosterone and estrogen, also affects mood and behavior, often leading to heightened emotions and sensitivity. Teenagers may experience intense feelings of happiness, sadness, anger, or frustration, sometimes without fully understanding why.

Cognitively, adolescence is a time of tremendous brain development. The prefrontal cortex, the area of the brain responsible for decision-making, impulse control, and planning, continues to mature well into the mid-20s. This means that while teenagers are capable of advanced thought processes, they may still struggle with impulse control and risk assessment. The brain's reward system is also particularly active during adolescence, making teenagers more prone to seeking out new and exciting experiences. This can sometimes lead to risky behaviors, such as experimenting with drugs or engaging in unsafe sexual activities, as teenagers are more likely to prioritize immediate rewards over long-term consequences.

Emotionally, adolescents are navigating the path to self-identity. They are trying to understand who they are, what they believe in, and where they fit in the world. This quest for identity often involves questioning authority, testing boundaries, and seeking independence from parents and caregivers. It is a crucial time for developing a sense of self and autonomy, but it can also be a period of significant confusion and turmoil. Teenagers may oscillate between wanting to be treated as adults and reverting to childlike behaviors when overwhelmed.

Socially, the adolescent years are marked by a shift in focus from family to peers. Friendships become increasingly important, and peer approval can heavily influence behavior and self-esteem. Teenagers may feel immense pressure to conform to peer group norms and standards, which can sometimes lead to conflicts with parents or teachers who may have different expectations. The need for acceptance and belonging is a powerful force in a teenager's life, driving many of their decisions and actions.

The role of technology and social media cannot be overlooked when understanding the modern adolescent mind. Teenagers today are digital natives, growing up in a world where social media and instant communication are the norms. While these platforms can provide valuable opportunities for connection and self-expression, they can also contribute to anxiety, depression, and a distorted sense of reality. The constant comparison to others, cyberbullying, and the pressure to maintain a certain online persona can be overwhelming for many teenagers.

Understanding the adolescent mind also involves recognizing the diverse experiences and challenges that different teenagers face. Factors such as gender, race, socioeconomic status, sexual orientation, and cultural background can all influence an adolescent's development and perspective. For example, LGBTQ+ teenagers may grapple with issues related to identity and acceptance in ways that their heterosexual peers do not. Similarly, adolescents from marginalized communities may face systemic barriers and discrimination that affect their mental health and opportunities.

To effectively support adolescents, it is essential to adopt a holistic approach that considers the interconnectedness of their physical, emotional, cognitive, and social development. Parents, educators, and caregivers play a crucial role in providing the guidance, support, and understanding that teenagers need during this critical period.

One key aspect of supporting adolescents is fostering open and honest communication. Teenagers need to feel that they can express their thoughts and feelings without fear of judgment or punishment. Active listening and validating their experiences are essential components of effective communication. This means taking the time to truly hear what they are saying, acknowledging their emotions, and offering empathy and support. It also involves being open to discussing difficult topics, such as mental health, sexuality, and substance use, in a non-judgmental and informative manner.

Setting clear and consistent boundaries is another important aspect of supporting adolescents. While teenagers seek independence, they also need structure and guidance to help them navigate the complexities of growing up. Establishing rules and expectations provides a sense of security and helps teenagers understand the consequences of their actions. However, it is equally important to involve them in the process of setting these boundaries, allowing for negotiation and compromise. This approach fosters a sense of responsibility and ownership over their behavior.

Encouraging positive peer relationships is also crucial. Parents and caregivers can support their teenagers by helping them develop healthy social skills and by being aware of their friends and social circles. Promoting activities that build self-esteem and confidence, such as sports, arts, or volunteer work, can help teenagers form positive identities and resist negative peer pressure.

Mental health is a critical area of focus when understanding the adolescent mind. The prevalence of anxiety, depression, and other mental health issues among teenagers is a growing concern. Early identification and intervention are key to addressing these challenges. Parents, teachers, and caregivers should be aware of the signs of mental health issues, such as changes in mood, behavior, or academic performance, and seek professional help when needed. Creating an environment where mental health is openly discussed and normalized can reduce stigma and encourage teenagers to seek help when they need it.

Empathy and patience are fundamental qualities for anyone working with adolescents. Understanding that the teenage years are inherently challenging and that teenagers are still developing the skills they need to manage their emotions and behaviors can help adults respond with compassion rather than frustration. Recognizing the unique strengths and potential of each teenager and providing opportunities for them to explore their interests and talents can foster a sense of purpose and motivation.

Lastly, it is essential to model the behavior and values you wish to instill in your teenager. Adolescents are highly observant and often learn more from what adults do than from what they say. Demonstrating healthy communication, self-care, responsibility, and empathy in your own life sets a powerful example for teenagers to follow.

Understanding the adolescent mind is a multifaceted and ongoing process that requires empathy, patience, and a willingness to adapt to the ever-changing needs of teenagers. By providing a supportive and nurturing environment, fostering open communication, setting clear boundaries, encouraging positive relationships, and being attuned to their mental health, we can help teenagers navigate the complexities of adolescence with grace and confidence.

ᐅᐅᐅ

"Adolescence is a time of profound growth and discovery. Embrace each challenge as an opportunity to learn and evolve. Remember, every setback is a step towards your true potential."

# TWO

## BUILDING TRUST AND CONNECTION

Building trust and connection with teenagers is a crucial yet challenging task that requires patience, empathy, and consistency. Trust is the foundation of any meaningful relationship, and for teenagers, it provides a sense of security and support that is essential for their emotional and psychological development. Connection, on the other hand, ensures that teenagers feel understood and valued, which can significantly impact their self-esteem and overall well-being.

Establishing trust begins with creating an environment where teenagers feel safe and respected. This means acknowledging their individuality and recognizing that their thoughts, feelings, and experiences are valid. One effective way to build this environment is through active listening. When teenagers feel heard, they are more likely to open up and share their inner worlds. Active listening involves more than just hearing the words; it requires paying full attention, making eye contact, and responding thoughtfully. It is about being present and showing genuine interest in what they are saying. This can be particularly challenging in a world filled with distractions, but making a conscious effort to listen can significantly strengthen the bond between parents or caregivers and teenagers.

Consistency is another vital component in building trust. Teenagers need to know that they can rely on the adults in their lives. This means being dependable and following through on promises and commitments. If a parent or caregiver consistently shows up when they say they will, it reinforces the teenager's belief that they can trust this person. Consistency also extends to setting and enforcing boundaries. Clear, consistent boundaries provide structure and security, helping teenagers understand what is expected of them and what they can expect from others. It is important to communicate these boundaries clearly and explain the reasoning behind them. When teenagers understand the purpose of rules and boundaries, they are more likely to respect them.

Honesty is a cornerstone of trust. Teenagers are perceptive and can often tell when they are being lied to or manipulated. Being honest, even when the truth is difficult, fosters respect and trust. This does not mean sharing every detail of adult life with a teenager but rather being transparent about issues that affect them directly. For example, if there are family challenges or financial difficulties, providing age-appropriate information can help teenagers feel included and respected. It also sets a positive example for them to follow in their own relationships.

Empathy is essential in building a strong connection with teenagers. Empathy involves understanding and sharing the feelings of another person. When parents and caregivers show empathy towards teenagers, it helps to validate their emotions and experiences. Teenagers often feel misunderstood or dismissed, so demonstrating empathy can bridge this gap. This means acknowledging their struggles and successes, expressing compassion, and offering support without judgment. It is about seeing the world from their perspective and responding with kindness and understanding.

Spending quality time together is another effective way to build trust and connection. Shared activities, whether it's a family game night, a walk in the park, or simply sitting down for a meal together, provide opportunities for bonding and open communication. These moments allow teenagers to feel valued and appreciated, reinforcing the connection. It is also important to be present during these times, setting aside distractions such as phones or work to fully engage with the teenager. Quality time does not have to be elaborate or time-consuming; even small, consistent interactions can make a significant difference.

Respecting a teenager's need for privacy is crucial in building trust. Adolescents are at a stage where they are developing their own identities and seeking independence. Respecting their privacy means giving them the space to grow and make their own decisions while still being available for support and guidance. This involves knocking before entering their room, not prying into their personal conversations or journals, and allowing them to have their own interests and friendships. When teenagers feel that their privacy is respected, they are more likely to trust and confide in the adults in their lives.

Encouraging open and honest communication is fundamental to building trust and connection. This involves creating a safe space where teenagers feel comfortable expressing their thoughts and feelings without fear of judgment or punishment. It is important to listen without interrupting, to ask open-ended questions that encourage deeper conversations, and to respond with empathy and understanding. It is also beneficial to model this behavior by being open and honest about your own thoughts and feelings, demonstrating that it is okay to be vulnerable and that communication is a two-way street.

Supporting teenagers in their interests and activities is another way to build a strong connection. Showing genuine interest in their hobbies, attending their events, and celebrating their achievements can make teenagers feel valued and supported. It is important to encourage their passions and provide opportunities for them to explore their interests. This not only strengthens the bond between parents and teenagers but also boosts their confidence and self-esteem.

Being patient and understanding during conflicts is crucial in maintaining trust and connection. Adolescence is a time of intense emotions and frequent conflicts, but how these conflicts are handled can significantly impact the relationship. It is important to stay calm, listen to their perspective, and work towards a resolution that respects both parties' feelings and needs. Apologizing when necessary and showing that you are willing to learn and grow from these experiences can also strengthen the relationship.

Providing consistent and unconditional support is essential for building trust. Teenagers need to know that they can rely on their parents or caregivers regardless of the circumstances. This means being there for them during difficult times, offering encouragement and guidance, and showing that your love and support are not contingent on their behavior or achievements. Knowing that they have a dependable support system can give teenagers the confidence to take risks and pursue their goals.

Encouraging autonomy and decision-making helps build trust and prepares teenagers for adulthood. Allowing them to make their own choices, even if it means making mistakes, shows that you trust their judgment and respect their independence. It is important to provide guidance and support but also to step back and allow them to learn from their experiences. This fosters a sense of responsibility and self-efficacy, reinforcing the trust and connection in the relationship.

Understanding and appreciating the individuality of each teenager is crucial. Every teenager is unique, with their own personality, interests, and challenges. Recognizing and celebrating these differences can help build a strong connection. It is important to avoid comparisons with siblings or peers and to focus on the teenager's individual strengths and qualities. This shows that you value them for who they are, which can significantly enhance their self-esteem and trust in the relationship.

Building trust and connection with teenagers is an ongoing process that requires effort, patience, and understanding. It is about creating an environment where they feel safe, respected, and valued, and where they can express themselves openly and honestly. It involves being consistent, honest, empathetic, and supportive, and respecting their need for privacy and independence. By focusing on these principles, parents and caregivers can build strong, trusting relationships with their teenagers that provide a solid foundation for their growth and development.

One practical approach to building trust is to engage in joint problem-solving. When issues arise, rather than imposing solutions, involve the teenager in the process of finding a resolution. This collaborative approach demonstrates respect for their input and fosters a sense of responsibility. It also provides an opportunity for teaching valuable problem-solving and decision-making skills. By working together to address challenges, parents and caregivers can reinforce the trust and connection in the relationship.

Another effective strategy is to practice forgiveness and understanding. Teenagers, like all people, make mistakes. It is important to approach these situations with a mindset of learning and growth rather than punishment and blame. By offering forgiveness and understanding, parents and caregivers can help teenagers learn from their mistakes and move forward in a positive direction. This approach also models the importance of compassion and empathy in relationships.

Encouraging self-expression is also crucial in building trust and connection. Providing opportunities for teenagers to express themselves through various outlets, such as art, music, writing, or sports, can help them explore their identities and develop their talents. It is important to support their creative endeavors and celebrate their achievements. This not only strengthens the bond between parents and teenagers but also boosts their confidence and self-esteem.

Building trust and connection with teenagers also involves fostering a sense of belonging. Teenagers need to feel that they are part of a supportive and loving community. This can be achieved by creating family traditions, participating in community activities, and fostering a sense of shared values and goals. When teenagers feel that they are part of a larger community, they are more likely to develop a strong sense of identity and purpose.

It is also important to recognize and address the impact of external influences on teenagers. Peer pressure, social media, and societal expectations can all affect a teenager's self-esteem and behavior. By maintaining open communication and providing guidance, parents and caregivers can help teenagers navigate these influences in a healthy and positive way. This involves discussing the potential risks and benefits of different influences and encouraging critical thinking and self-reflection.

Finally, building trust and connection with teenagers involves being a positive role model. Teenagers are observant and often look to the adults in their lives for cues on how to behave and interact with others. By demonstrating positive behaviors, such as effective communication, empathy, responsibility, and resilience, parents and caregivers can provide a powerful example for teenagers to follow. This modeling reinforces the values and principles that are important for building strong, trusting relationships.

In conclusion, building trust and connection with teenagers is a multifaceted process that requires dedication, empathy, and consistency. It is about creating an environment where they feel safe, respected, and valued, and where they can express themselves openly and honestly. By focusing on active listening, consistency, honesty, empathy, quality time, respect for privacy, open communication, support for interests, patience during conflicts, unconditional support, encouragement of autonomy, appreciation of individuality, joint problem-solving, forgiveness, self-expression, fostering belonging, addressing external influences, and positive role modeling, parents and caregivers can build strong, trusting relationships with their teenagers. These relationships provide a solid foundation for the teenager's growth and development, helping them navigate the complexities of adolescence with confidence and resilience.

ᗡᗡᗡ

"Empathy is the cornerstone of understanding. By seeing the world through another's eyes, we build bridges of compassion and trust. Let empathy guide your interactions and shape your relationships."

# THREE

## EFFECTIVE COMMUNICATION SKILLS

Effective communication skills are essential in fostering strong, healthy relationships with teenagers. Communication is more than just exchanging words; it is about understanding, connecting, and building a rapport that allows for open and honest dialogue. Mastering the art of communication with teenagers involves a combination of listening, speaking, and nonverbal skills that together create an environment of trust and mutual respect.

One of the most fundamental aspects of effective communication is active listening. Active listening means giving full attention to the speaker, understanding their message, responding thoughtfully, and remembering what was said. For teenagers, feeling heard and understood is crucial. When parents and caregivers practice active listening, they demonstrate that they value their teenager's thoughts and feelings. This involves not just hearing the words but also paying attention to the emotions behind them. Nodding, maintaining eye contact, and providing verbal acknowledgments like "I see" or "I understand" can make teenagers feel validated and respected.

In addition to active listening, asking open-ended questions is a powerful tool in effective communication. Open-ended questions encourage teenagers to express themselves more fully and think critically about their responses. Instead of asking questions that can be answered with a simple "yes" or "no," such as "Did you have a good day?" try asking, "What was the best part of your day?" or "How did you feel about your presentation?" These types of questions invite teenagers to share more about their experiences and feelings, fostering deeper conversations and a better understanding of their perspective.

Another important aspect of effective communication is expressing empathy. Empathy involves understanding and sharing the feelings of another person. When communicating with teenagers, showing empathy helps to build trust and rapport. This can be achieved by acknowledging their feelings and experiences without judgment. For instance, if a teenager is upset about a conflict with a friend, a parent might say, "I can see that you're really upset about what happened. That must have been really hard for you." This type of response shows that the parent is not only listening but also cares about the teenager's emotional experience.

Nonverbal communication also plays a significant role in how messages are conveyed and received. Body language, facial expressions, and tone of voice can all impact the effectiveness of communication. Positive nonverbal cues, such as maintaining eye contact, nodding, and leaning slightly forward, can convey interest and attentiveness. Conversely, negative nonverbal cues, such as crossing arms, looking away, or using a harsh tone, can create barriers to effective communication. Being mindful of these nonverbal signals and ensuring they align with the verbal message is essential in creating a supportive and open communication environment.

Another key element of effective communication with teenagers is clarity and conciseness. Teenagers, like everyone else, can become overwhelmed or confused by long, complicated explanations. It is important to convey messages in a clear, straightforward manner. This involves being direct and to the point while avoiding unnecessary jargon or overly complex language. For example, instead of saying, "You need to be more conscientious about managing your time effectively because it will have a significant impact on your academic performance and future opportunities," you might say, "Try to manage your time better so you can do well in school and have more options later."

Consistency is also important in communication. Consistent messages help teenagers understand expectations and boundaries, providing a sense of stability and security. This means not only being consistent in what is said but also in how it is said and enforced. Mixed messages can lead to confusion and mistrust. For example, if a parent consistently emphasizes the importance of honesty but reacts angrily when the teenager tells the truth about a mistake, it can create a conflicting message. Ensuring that actions align with words reinforces the communicated values and expectations.

Effective communication also involves being open to feedback and willing to adjust as necessary. Communication is a two-way street, and teenagers should feel that their input is valued and considered. This means being open to hearing their perspective, even if it differs from your own, and being willing to adjust your approach if needed. For example, if a teenager expresses that they feel overwhelmed by too many activities, a parent might need to reevaluate and discuss how to balance their schedule better. This shows that their feelings and opinions matter and that you are willing to work together to find solutions.

Encouraging self-expression is another important aspect of effective communication. Teenagers need to feel that they can express themselves freely without fear of judgment or ridicule. This involves creating a safe space where they can share their thoughts, feelings, and experiences openly. It also means being supportive of their individuality and interests.

For instance, if a teenager is passionate about a particular hobby or activity, showing interest and support can foster a sense of acceptance and validation. Encouraging self-expression helps teenagers develop a strong sense of identity and self-worth, which are crucial for their overall well-being.

Effective communication also requires managing emotions, both your own and your teenager's. Adolescence is a time of intense emotions, and conflicts are bound to arise. How these conflicts are handled can significantly impact the relationship. It is important to stay calm and composed, even in heated situations. Taking a moment to breathe and collect your thoughts before responding can prevent escalating the conflict.

It is also helpful to model healthy emotional regulation by demonstrating how to manage stress and frustration constructively. This can include techniques such as deep breathing, taking a break, or using "I" statements to express feelings without blaming or criticizing the other person. For example, saying, "I feel frustrated when the chores aren't done because it adds to my workload," is more constructive than saying, "You never do your chores."

Setting aside regular times for meaningful conversations can also enhance communication with teenagers. Busy schedules and daily distractions can make it difficult to find time for in-depth discussions. Setting aside regular time, such as during meals or before bed, can create opportunities for meaningful conversations. These moments can help strengthen the connection and ensure that communication remains a priority. It is also important to be flexible and open to spontaneous conversations, as teenagers may choose to open up at unexpected times.

In addition to regular conversations, it is beneficial to use different communication methods to connect with teenagers. While face-to-face conversations are ideal, sometimes teenagers may feel more comfortable expressing themselves through writing, texting, or other forms of digital communication. Being open to these different methods can help bridge the communication gap and ensure that teenagers feel heard and understood.

For example, if a teenager finds it difficult to talk about a sensitive topic in person, they might feel more comfortable writing a letter or sending a message. Respecting their preferred method of communication can foster a sense of trust and openness.

Building effective communication skills also involves understanding and respecting cultural differences. Cultural background can significantly influence communication styles and expectations. Being aware of and sensitive to these differences can help foster better communication.

For example, some cultures place a high value on respect for authority and may have different norms around how to express disagreement or emotions. Understanding these cultural nuances can help parents and caregivers communicate more effectively and respectfully with their teenagers.

Providing positive reinforcement and constructive feedback is also crucial in effective communication. Acknowledging and praising positive behavior and efforts can boost a teenager's confidence and motivation. Constructive feedback, on the other hand, should be specific, focused on behavior rather than character, and delivered in a way that encourages growth and improvement. For example, instead of saying, "You're so lazy," it is more effective to say, "I've noticed that you've been struggling to keep up with your homework. Let's talk about how we can create a better study plan."

Effective communication with teenagers also involves setting realistic expectations and being patient. Teenagers are still developing their communication skills, and it is important to be patient and understanding as they navigate this process. Setting realistic expectations means recognizing that there will be challenges and setbacks, but also celebrating progress and growth. Patience is key in maintaining a supportive and open communication environment, even when conversations are difficult or frustrating.

Lastly, self-awareness and reflection are essential components of effective communication. Taking the time to reflect on your own communication style, strengths, and areas for improvement can help enhance your interactions with teenagers.

This involves being honest with yourself about any biases or habits that may hinder effective communication and being willing to make changes. Self-awareness also includes recognizing your own emotional triggers and learning how to manage them constructively. By continually reflecting on and improving your communication skills, you can foster stronger, healthier relationships with the teenagers in your life.

In conclusion, effective communication skills are vital for building strong, healthy relationships with teenagers. It involves a combination of active listening, empathy, nonverbal communication, clarity, consistency, openness to feedback, encouragement of self-expression, emotional regulation, regular conversations, use of different communication methods, cultural sensitivity, positive reinforcement, realistic expectations, patience, and self-awareness.

By mastering these skills, parents and caregivers can create an environment of trust and mutual respect, fostering open and honest dialogue that supports the emotional and psychological development of teenagers. These communication skills not only enhance the relationship but also provide teenagers with valuable tools for navigating their own relationships and challenges in life.

"A supportive home is the foundation for a teenager's success. Provide a space filled with love, patience, and understanding. This environment will nurture their growth and resilience."

# FOUR

## EMBRACING CHANGE

Embracing change is a fundamental aspect of navigating the journey of adolescence. Change during this period is inevitable, encompassing a wide array of physical, emotional, cognitive, and social transformations. For teenagers, understanding and adapting to these changes is crucial for their development and well-being. Embracing change involves not only accepting the inevitability of growth and transformation but also actively engaging with it in a positive and proactive manner.

Physically, adolescence is marked by puberty, a time when the body undergoes significant changes. These changes include the development of secondary sexual characteristics, such as the growth of breasts in girls and the deepening of voices in boys, as well as increases in height and muscle mass. These physical transformations can be both exciting and challenging for teenagers. On one hand, they signify the transition from childhood to adulthood, bringing a sense of maturity and independence. On the other hand, they can also lead to feelings of self-consciousness and insecurity as teenagers adjust to their changing bodies. Embracing these physical changes involves fostering a positive body image and self-acceptance. Encouraging teenagers to view their bodies with appreciation and respect, rather than comparison and criticism, can help them navigate this period with confidence.

Emotionally, adolescence is a time of heightened sensitivity and intense feelings. Hormonal changes can lead to mood swings, making teenagers more susceptible to feelings of happiness, sadness, anger, and frustration. These emotional fluctuations are a normal part of development, but they can be overwhelming. Embracing emotional change means recognizing and validating these feelings rather than dismissing them. It is important for teenagers to learn that their emotions are valid and that it is okay to feel a wide range of feelings. Providing them with tools to manage their emotions, such as mindfulness practices, journaling, or talking to a trusted adult, can help them develop emotional resilience. Encouraging open communication about emotions and creating a supportive environment where teenagers feel safe to express their feelings can also make a significant difference.

Cognitively, adolescence is a period of significant brain development. The prefrontal cortex, which is responsible for decision-making, impulse control, and planning, continues to mature throughout the teenage years. This ongoing development means that teenagers are capable of more complex thought processes but may still struggle with impulse control and risk assessment. Embracing cognitive change involves encouraging critical thinking and problem-solving skills. This can be achieved by providing opportunities for teenagers to engage in activities that challenge their minds, such as puzzles, strategy games, or debates. Encouraging them to think critically about the information they encounter, whether in school, on social media, or in conversations, helps them develop their cognitive abilities. It is also important to provide guidance and support as they navigate the decision-making process, helping them to weigh the pros and cons and consider the potential consequences of their actions.

Socially, adolescence is characterized by a shift in focus from family to peers. Friendships become increasingly important, and teenagers often seek approval and acceptance from their peer group. This can lead to changes in behavior and attitudes as they strive to fit in and be accepted. Embracing social change means recognizing the importance of peer relationships while also maintaining strong family connections. It involves supporting teenagers in building healthy, positive friendships and providing guidance on how to navigate peer pressure. Encouraging involvement in extracurricular activities, such as sports, clubs, or volunteer work, can help teenagers develop social skills and build a supportive network of peers. It is also important to maintain open lines of communication, allowing teenagers to share their experiences and seek advice when needed.

In addition to these developmental changes, teenagers also face changes in their environments and circumstances. This can include transitions such as moving to a new school, changes in family dynamics, or shifts in societal expectations. Embracing these external changes involves developing adaptability and resilience. Helping teenagers to view change as an opportunity for growth and learning, rather than a threat, can foster a positive mindset. Encouraging a sense of curiosity and openness to new experiences can help them navigate these transitions with confidence. Providing practical support, such as helping them develop organizational skills or teaching them how to manage stress, can also make a significant difference.

One key aspect of embracing change is developing a growth mindset. A growth mindset is the belief that abilities and intelligence can be developed through effort, learning, and perseverance. This mindset contrasts with a fixed mindset, which holds that abilities are static and unchangeable. Encouraging teenagers to adopt a growth mindset can help them embrace change with a positive attitude. This involves praising effort rather than innate talent, encouraging them to take on challenges, and viewing mistakes as opportunities for learning. By fostering a growth mindset, teenagers can develop the resilience and determination needed to navigate change successfully.

Embracing change also involves developing self-awareness. Self-awareness is the ability to reflect on one's thoughts, feelings, and behaviors and understand how they impact oneself and others. It is a crucial skill for personal growth and development. Encouraging teenagers to engage in self-reflection, whether through journaling, meditation, or conversations with trusted adults, can help them develop a deeper understanding of themselves. This self-awareness can lead to greater self-acceptance and the ability to navigate change with confidence and clarity.

Another important aspect of embracing change is building a support system. Having a network of supportive friends, family members, and mentors can provide a sense of security and stability during times of change. Encouraging teenagers to build and maintain these relationships can help them feel connected and supported. It is also important for parents and caregivers to be a consistent source of support, offering guidance and encouragement while also respecting the teenager's growing independence.

Practicing self-care is also essential in navigating change. Change can be stressful, and it is important for teenagers to have strategies in place to manage this stress. Encouraging them to engage in activities that promote physical, emotional, and mental well-being, such as exercise, hobbies, or relaxation techniques, can help them build resilience. Teaching them the importance of self-care and providing opportunities for them to practice it can help them develop healthy habits that will serve them throughout their lives.

Embracing change also involves being open to new perspectives and experiences. Encouraging teenagers to step out of their comfort zones and try new things can help them develop a broader understanding of the world and themselves. This can include exploring different cultures, trying new activities, or meeting new people. Being open to new experiences fosters a sense of curiosity and adaptability, which are important skills for navigating change.

It is also important to recognize and celebrate the milestones and achievements that come with change. Whether it is starting high school, learning to drive, or graduating, acknowledging these accomplishments can help teenagers feel a sense of pride and motivation. Celebrating these moments reinforces the idea that change is a natural and positive part of life.

Embracing change is not just about accepting what happens but actively engaging with it in a positive and proactive way. It involves developing the skills and mindset needed to navigate change successfully. By fostering a growth mindset, developing self-awareness, building a support system, practicing self-care, being open to new experiences, and celebrating achievements, teenagers can learn to embrace change with confidence and resilience.

Parents and caregivers play a crucial role in helping teenagers embrace change. Providing a stable and supportive environment, offering guidance and encouragement, and being a positive role model can all make a significant difference. It is important to communicate openly and honestly about changes, whether they are personal, familial, or societal, and to involve teenagers in the decision-making process when appropriate. This helps them feel a sense of control and agency, which can reduce anxiety and build confidence.

Embracing change is an ongoing process that requires patience, empathy, and support. It involves recognizing the challenges and opportunities that come with change and helping teenagers develop the skills and mindset needed to navigate these transitions successfully. By embracing change, teenagers can develop the resilience, adaptability, and confidence needed to thrive in an ever-changing world.

ᐁᐁᐁ

"Healthy communication is the key to strong relationships. Listen actively and speak with kindness. Open dialogue fosters trust and mutual respect."

# FIVE

## ENCOURAGING INDEPENDENCE

Encouraging independence in teenagers is a crucial aspect of their development. It involves helping them build the skills, confidence, and mindset necessary to become self-reliant and responsible adults. Independence is not just about allowing teenagers to do things on their own; it is about fostering a sense of autonomy, self-efficacy, and resilience that will serve them throughout their lives.

The process of encouraging independence begins with creating an environment that supports and nurtures growth. This environment should be one where teenagers feel safe to explore, make mistakes, and learn from their experiences. Parents and caregivers play a vital role in establishing this supportive atmosphere by providing guidance, setting boundaries, and offering encouragement while also allowing space for self-discovery. It is important to strike a balance between offering support and stepping back to let teenagers take the lead in their own lives.

One of the key aspects of fostering independence is building self-confidence. Teenagers need to believe in their own abilities and trust that they can handle challenges and setbacks. Parents and caregivers can help build this confidence by providing opportunities for teenagers to succeed and by acknowledging their efforts and achievements. This involves praising not just the outcome but also the process and the effort they put into their endeavors. For instance, acknowledging the hard work and dedication a teenager shows in preparing for a school project, regardless of the final grade, reinforces the value of perseverance and effort.

Encouraging teenagers to take on responsibilities is another important step in fostering independence. This can include tasks such as managing their own schedules, handling chores, or making decisions about their personal lives. Giving teenagers the responsibility to manage these aspects of their lives helps them develop important life skills, such as time management, organization, and decision-making. It also teaches them the importance of accountability and the consequences of their actions. Allowing them to experience the natural consequences of their decisions, whether positive or negative, is a valuable learning opportunity. For example, if a teenager chooses not to complete their homework and receives a poor grade, this consequence reinforces the importance of fulfilling responsibilities.

Providing opportunities for problem-solving is another way to encourage independence. When faced with challenges, teenagers should be encouraged to think critically and come up with solutions on their own. This involves asking open-ended questions that guide them to consider different options and the potential outcomes of each. For instance, if a teenager is struggling with a conflict with a friend, asking questions like "What do you think would happen if you talked to them about how you feel?" or "What other ways could you approach this situation?" helps them develop problem-solving skills and encourages them to take ownership of their decisions.

Allowing teenagers to make choices about their lives is a fundamental aspect of fostering independence. This involves giving them the freedom to make decisions about their interests, hobbies, and social activities. Supporting their choices, even if they differ from your own preferences, shows that you respect their autonomy and trust their judgment. It is important to provide guidance and set boundaries, but within those limits, teenagers should have the freedom to make their own choices and learn from their experiences. For example, if a teenager expresses an interest in trying a new sport or hobby, encouraging them to pursue it and supporting their efforts, even if it is something unfamiliar to you, fosters a sense of independence and self-discovery.

Teaching financial responsibility is another crucial aspect of encouraging independence. Helping teenagers understand the value of money, how to budget, and the importance of saving and spending wisely prepares them for financial independence in adulthood. This can involve giving them an allowance, encouraging them to save for things they want, or helping them find part-time jobs. Providing guidance on how to manage their money, such as setting up a bank account or creating a budget, helps them develop practical financial skills. It is also important to discuss the responsibilities that come with managing money, such as paying bills or understanding the consequences of debt. These lessons help teenagers develop a sense of financial responsibility and independence.

Encouraging independence also involves fostering a growth mindset. A growth mindset is the belief that abilities and intelligence can be developed through effort, learning, and perseverance. This mindset helps teenagers approach challenges with a positive attitude and a willingness to learn from their experiences. Encouraging a growth mindset involves praising effort and persistence rather than innate talent, and viewing mistakes as opportunities for growth rather than failures. For example, if a teenager struggles with a particular subject in school, praising their effort and encouraging them to keep trying and seek help when needed reinforces the value of persistence and resilience.

Supporting teenagers in developing self-care routines is another important aspect of fostering independence. Teaching them the importance of maintaining their physical, emotional, and mental well-being helps them develop healthy habits that will serve them throughout their lives. This can include encouraging regular exercise, healthy eating, adequate sleep, and relaxation techniques. It is also important to support their emotional and mental well-being by encouraging them to engage in activities they enjoy, practice mindfulness, and seek help when needed. Teaching teenagers to prioritize self-care helps them develop a sense of responsibility for their own well-being and fosters independence.

Building a supportive network is crucial for encouraging independence. Teenagers need to have a network of supportive friends, family members, and mentors who can provide guidance and encouragement. Encouraging teenagers to build and maintain these relationships helps them develop a sense of community and support. It is also important for parents and caregivers to be a consistent source of support, offering guidance and encouragement while also respecting the teenager's growing independence. This involves being available to listen and provide advice when needed, but also stepping back to allow the teenager to take the lead in their own lives.

Encouraging teenagers to set goals and work towards them is another important aspect of fostering independence. Goal setting helps teenagers develop a sense of purpose and direction and teaches them the value of planning and perseverance. Encouraging them to set realistic and achievable goals, and supporting them in developing a plan to achieve those goals, helps them develop important life skills. It is also important to celebrate their achievements and acknowledge their progress, reinforcing the value of hard work and dedication.

Encouraging independence also involves teaching teenagers to advocate for themselves. This means helping them develop the confidence and skills to speak up for their needs and rights. Encouraging them to express their opinions, ask for help when needed, and stand up for themselves in various situations fosters a sense of empowerment and self-efficacy. It is important to provide opportunities for teenagers to practice these skills, whether in school, with friends, or in other settings. Teaching them the importance of effective communication, assertiveness, and self-advocacy helps them navigate challenges and build a sense of independence.

Providing opportunities for teenagers to explore their interests and passions is another important aspect of fostering independence. Encouraging them to try new activities, explore different hobbies, and pursue their passions helps them develop a sense of identity and self-discovery. It is important to support their interests and provide opportunities for them to engage in activities that they enjoy and find meaningful. This helps them develop a sense of autonomy and independence, and fosters a sense of purpose and fulfillment.

Encouraging independence also involves helping teenagers develop a sense of responsibility and accountability. This means teaching them the importance of fulfilling their commitments, taking responsibility for their actions, and understanding the consequences of their behavior. Providing opportunities for teenagers to take on responsibilities, such as managing their own schedules, handling chores, or making decisions about their personal lives, helps them develop these important life skills. It is also important to hold them accountable for their actions and help them understand the consequences of their behavior, whether positive or negative. This reinforces the importance of responsibility and accountability and helps them develop a sense of independence.

Encouraging independence is an ongoing process that requires patience, empathy, and support. It involves creating an environment that supports and nurtures growth, building self-confidence, providing opportunities for problem-solving and decision-making, teaching financial responsibility, fostering a growth mindset, supporting self-care, building a supportive network, encouraging goal setting, teaching self-advocacy, and providing opportunities for exploration and responsibility. By fostering these skills and mindsets, parents and caregivers can help teenagers develop the independence and resilience needed to navigate the challenges of adolescence and adulthood.

ϸϸϸ

"Independence and responsibility go hand in hand. Encourage teenagers to take charge of their actions and decisions. This empowerment builds confidence and prepares them for adulthood."

# SIX
## MANAGING CONFLICTS PEACEFULLY

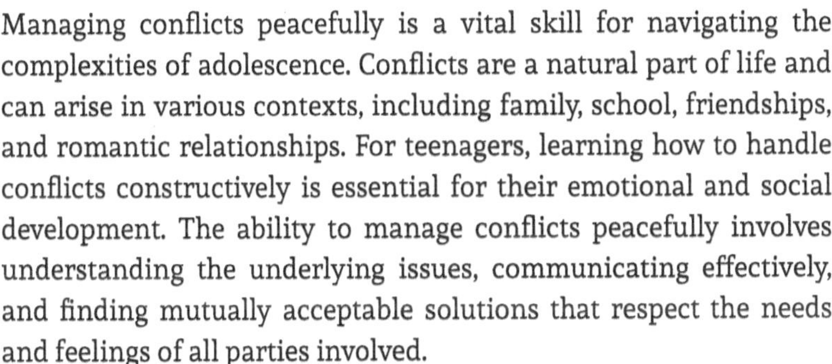

Managing conflicts peacefully is a vital skill for navigating the complexities of adolescence. Conflicts are a natural part of life and can arise in various contexts, including family, school, friendships, and romantic relationships. For teenagers, learning how to handle conflicts constructively is essential for their emotional and social development. The ability to manage conflicts peacefully involves understanding the underlying issues, communicating effectively, and finding mutually acceptable solutions that respect the needs and feelings of all parties involved.

One of the first steps in managing conflicts peacefully is understanding the root causes of the disagreement. Conflicts often arise from misunderstandings, differing perspectives, unmet needs, or emotional triggers. For teenagers, conflicts may be influenced by developmental changes, such as the quest for independence, identity exploration, and heightened sensitivity to peer relationships. Recognizing these underlying factors can help in addressing the core issues rather than just the surface symptoms.

It is important to approach conflicts with an open mind and a willingness to understand the other person's perspective. This involves active listening, empathy, and patience, which are crucial for creating an environment where all parties feel heard and respected.

Effective communication is a cornerstone of peaceful conflict resolution. Clear and open communication helps to prevent misunderstandings and ensures that everyone's needs and feelings are expressed and acknowledged. For teenagers, developing communication skills involves learning how to articulate their thoughts and emotions in a constructive manner. This can be challenging, especially in the heat of the moment, but it is essential for resolving conflicts peacefully. Encouraging teenagers to use "I" statements rather than "you" statements can help to reduce defensiveness and blame. For example, saying "I feel hurt when my opinions are dismissed" is more constructive than saying "You never listen to me." This approach helps to focus on the impact of the behavior rather than attacking the person, which can lead to a more productive dialogue.

Another important aspect of managing conflicts peacefully is learning how to regulate emotions. Adolescence is a time of heightened emotions, and conflicts can easily escalate if emotions are not managed effectively. Teaching teenagers techniques for emotional regulation, such as deep breathing, mindfulness, or taking a time-out, can help them stay calm and composed during disagreements. It is important to recognize that strong emotions, such as anger, frustration, or sadness, are normal and valid, but it is how these emotions are expressed that matters. Encouraging teenagers to take a moment to collect their thoughts before responding can prevent impulsive reactions that may exacerbate the conflict.

Finding mutually acceptable solutions is a key goal of peaceful conflict resolution. This involves negotiating and compromising to reach an agreement that satisfies the needs of all parties involved. For teenagers, learning how to negotiate and compromise is an important life skill that fosters cooperation and respect. It is important to approach negotiations with a collaborative mindset, focusing on finding solutions rather than winning the argument. Encouraging teenagers to brainstorm possible solutions together and evaluate the pros and cons of each option can help them develop critical thinking and problem-solving skills. It is also important to ensure that the agreed-upon solution is fair and equitable, and that everyone's needs and concerns are addressed.

Building empathy is another essential component of managing conflicts peacefully. Empathy involves understanding and sharing the feelings of others, which can help to create a sense of connection and mutual respect. For teenagers, developing empathy involves putting themselves in the other person's shoes and considering how their actions and words may impact others. This can be challenging, especially when emotions are running high, but it is crucial for resolving conflicts constructively. Encouraging teenagers to express empathy by acknowledging the other person's feelings and validating their experiences can help to de-escalate tensions and create a more collaborative atmosphere.

Setting clear boundaries is also important for managing conflicts peacefully. Boundaries help to define acceptable behavior and ensure that everyone's rights and needs are respected. For teenagers, learning to set and respect boundaries is an important aspect of their development. This involves communicating their own boundaries clearly and assertively, as well as respecting the boundaries of others. For example, if a teenager feels uncomfortable with a friend's behavior, they might say, "I need some space right now. Can we talk about this later?" Setting boundaries helps to prevent conflicts from escalating and ensures that everyone feels safe and respected.

Developing conflict resolution skills also involves learning how to apologize and forgive. Apologizing when appropriate shows accountability and a willingness to make amends. For teenagers, learning to apologize involves acknowledging their role in the conflict and expressing genuine remorse. It is important to teach teenagers that apologizing is not a sign of weakness, but rather a sign of maturity and responsibility. Forgiveness, on the other hand, involves letting go of resentment and moving forward. Encouraging teenagers to forgive others and themselves can help to heal relationships and reduce the emotional burden of conflicts.

It is also important to recognize that not all conflicts can be resolved immediately, and some may require ongoing effort and dialogue. For teenagers, understanding that conflict resolution is a process rather than a one-time event can help to manage expectations and reduce frustration. It is important to be patient and persistent, and to continue working towards a resolution even if progress is slow. Providing support and encouragement throughout this process can help teenagers stay committed to finding a peaceful resolution.

Creating a positive and supportive environment is crucial for fostering peaceful conflict resolution. This involves promoting a culture of respect, empathy, and cooperation in all areas of life, including family, school, and peer relationships. For parents and caregivers, modeling positive conflict resolution behaviors is an important way to teach teenagers how to handle conflicts constructively. Demonstrating how to communicate effectively, regulate emotions, and find mutually acceptable solutions sets a positive example for teenagers to follow. It is also important to create opportunities for teenagers to practice these skills in a safe and supportive environment, whether through family discussions, role-playing exercises, or conflict resolution workshops.

In addition to developing interpersonal conflict resolution skills, it is important for teenagers to learn how to manage internal conflicts. Internal conflicts, such as conflicting desires, values, or goals, can create significant stress and anxiety. Encouraging teenagers to engage in self-reflection and introspection can help them understand and resolve these internal conflicts. This involves exploring their thoughts and feelings, identifying the sources of conflict, and considering possible solutions. Providing support and guidance through this process can help teenagers develop greater self-awareness and emotional resilience.

Education and awareness are also important for managing conflicts peacefully. Teaching teenagers about different conflict resolution strategies, such as mediation, negotiation, and collaborative problem-solving, provides them with a toolkit of skills to draw upon in various situations. It is also important to raise awareness about the impact of conflict on mental and emotional well-being, and to encourage teenagers to seek help and support when needed. Providing access to resources, such as counseling services, support groups, or conflict resolution training programs, can help teenagers develop the skills and confidence needed to manage conflicts constructively.

Encouraging a growth mindset is another important aspect of managing conflicts peacefully. A growth mindset involves viewing conflicts as opportunities for learning and growth rather than as threats or failures. Encouraging teenagers to adopt a growth mindset helps them approach conflicts with a positive and proactive attitude. This involves recognizing that conflicts are a normal part of life, and that they can provide valuable lessons and opportunities for personal development. By viewing conflicts as opportunities for growth, teenagers can develop greater resilience and adaptability, and learn to navigate challenges with confidence and grace.

Finally, fostering a sense of community and connectedness can help to create a supportive environment for peaceful conflict resolution.

Encouraging teenagers to build positive relationships and develop a sense of belonging can reduce feelings of isolation and increase their willingness to engage in constructive conflict resolution. This involves promoting inclusivity, diversity, and mutual respect in all areas of life. Creating opportunities for teenagers to connect with others, whether through social activities, community service, or group projects, helps to build a sense of community and support.

In conclusion, managing conflicts peacefully is a multifaceted process that involves understanding the root causes of conflicts, communicating effectively, regulating emotions, finding mutually acceptable solutions, building empathy, setting clear boundaries, apologizing and forgiving, and fostering a positive and supportive environment. It requires patience, persistence, and a willingness to engage in ongoing dialogue and reflection. By developing these skills and mindsets, teenagers can learn to navigate conflicts constructively and build stronger, healthier relationships. Encouraging a growth mindset, providing education and resources, and fostering a sense of community and connectedness are also important aspects of promoting peaceful conflict resolution. Through these efforts, teenagers can develop the resilience, adaptability, and confidence needed to handle conflicts with grace and maturity.

ppp

*"Understanding the adolescent mind requires patience and empathy. Recognize the unique challenges they face. Support them with guidance and compassion."*

# SEVEN
## SUPPORTING ACADEMIC SUCCESS

Supporting academic success in teenagers is a multifaceted endeavor that involves fostering a positive learning environment, encouraging effective study habits, and providing emotional and practical support. The teenage years are a critical period for academic development, as students navigate increasingly challenging coursework, prepare for higher education or career paths, and develop the skills necessary for lifelong learning. To support teenagers in achieving academic success, parents, educators, and caregivers must work collaboratively to create an environment that promotes motivation, resilience, and a love of learning.

A positive learning environment is essential for academic success. This begins at home, where parents and caregivers can create a space that is conducive to studying and learning. This space should be quiet, well-lit, and free from distractions such as television and loud noises. Providing the necessary supplies, such as textbooks, notebooks, and a reliable internet connection, ensures that teenagers have the tools they need to succeed. Additionally, establishing a routine that includes regular study times can help teenagers develop good habits and maintain a consistent schedule.

Encouraging a balance between academic responsibilities and leisure activities is also important, as it helps prevent burnout and promotes overall well-being.

Effective communication between parents, teachers, and students is another key component of supporting academic success. Parents and caregivers should maintain open lines of communication with their teenager's teachers and school staff to stay informed about their progress and any potential challenges. Attending parent-teacher conferences, participating in school events, and staying engaged in the school community can help parents better understand their teenager's academic experience and provide the necessary support. Encouraging teenagers to communicate with their teachers and seek help when needed fosters a sense of responsibility and self-advocacy. It is important for teenagers to feel comfortable asking questions and expressing concerns, as this can lead to a deeper understanding of the material and improved academic performance.

Encouraging effective study habits is crucial for academic success. Teaching teenagers how to organize their time and manage their workload helps them develop important skills that will serve them throughout their lives. Time management techniques, such as creating a study schedule, setting goals, and breaking tasks into manageable chunks, can help teenagers stay on track and avoid procrastination. Encouraging the use of planners or digital tools to keep track of assignments, tests, and deadlines can also be beneficial. Additionally, teaching teenagers to prioritize their tasks and focus on the most important or challenging assignments first can help them make the most of their study time.

Developing strong study skills is another important aspect of academic success. This includes teaching teenagers how to take effective notes, review and retain information, and prepare for exams. Different students have different learning styles, so it is important to help teenagers identify the study methods that work best for them. For some, this may involve creating flashcards, while others may benefit from summarizing information in their own words or teaching the material to someone else. Encouraging teenagers to find a study routine that suits their learning style can help them retain information more effectively and perform better on exams.

Providing emotional support is equally important in supporting academic success. The teenage years can be a stressful and challenging time, and academic pressures can contribute to anxiety and burnout. It is important for parents and caregivers to be attuned to their teenager's emotional well-being and provide support when needed. This includes offering encouragement and praise for their efforts and achievements, as well as being understanding and supportive during times of struggle. Encouraging a growth mindset, which emphasizes the value of effort and learning from mistakes, can help teenagers develop resilience and perseverance. By focusing on the process rather than just the outcome, parents and caregivers can help teenagers build confidence and a positive attitude towards learning.

Encouraging a love of learning is another important aspect of supporting academic success. When teenagers are motivated and passionate about what they are learning, they are more likely to engage with the material and perform well academically. Parents and caregivers can foster a love of learning by exposing teenagers to a variety of subjects and experiences, both inside and outside of school. This can include visiting museums, attending cultural events, or exploring different hobbies and interests. Encouraging teenagers to pursue their passions and explore new areas of interest helps them develop a well-rounded education and a lifelong love of learning.

Supporting academic success also involves addressing any potential barriers to learning. This can include identifying and addressing learning disabilities, providing additional support for students who are struggling, and ensuring that teenagers have access to the resources they need to succeed. For students with learning disabilities, individualized education plans (IEPs) or 504 plans can provide the necessary accommodations and support to help them succeed academically. It is important for parents, educators, and caregivers to work together to identify any potential challenges and develop strategies to address them.

In addition to providing support at home, extracurricular activities and enrichment programs can also play a significant role in supporting academic success. Participation in activities such as sports, music, art, or academic clubs can help teenagers develop important skills, build confidence, and foster a sense of belonging. These activities can also provide opportunities for teenagers to apply what they have learned in the classroom in new and creative ways. Encouraging teenagers to participate in extracurricular activities that interest them can help them develop a well-rounded education and enhance their academic experience.

Mentorship and tutoring programs can also be valuable resources for supporting academic success. Having a mentor or tutor who can provide guidance, support, and additional instruction can help teenagers navigate academic challenges and develop their skills. Mentorship programs can also provide valuable role models and help teenagers build connections and networks that can support their academic and career goals. Encouraging teenagers to seek out mentorship and tutoring opportunities can provide them with additional support and resources to help them succeed.

It is also important to recognize the role of physical health in supporting academic success. A healthy lifestyle, including regular exercise, a balanced diet, and adequate sleep, can have a significant impact on a teenager's ability to focus, learn, and perform academically. Encouraging teenagers to take care of their physical health by getting enough sleep, eating nutritious meals, and staying active can help them maintain the energy and focus they need to succeed in school. Additionally, promoting healthy habits, such as taking regular breaks during study sessions and practicing relaxation techniques, can help reduce stress and improve overall well-being.

Parents and caregivers can also support academic success by modeling positive behaviors and attitudes towards learning. Demonstrating a love of learning, curiosity, and a willingness to explore new ideas can inspire teenagers to develop similar attitudes. Sharing personal experiences and stories about overcoming challenges and achieving goals can also provide valuable lessons and motivation for teenagers. By setting a positive example and showing that learning is a lifelong journey, parents and caregivers can help teenagers develop a positive attitude towards education and a commitment to academic success.

Finally, it is important to recognize that academic success is not solely defined by grades and test scores. While these are important measures of academic performance, they do not capture the full scope of a teenager's abilities and potential. Academic success also includes the development of critical thinking skills, creativity, problem-solving abilities, and a passion for learning. Encouraging teenagers to focus on their overall development and growth, rather than just their grades, helps them build a more holistic and meaningful understanding of academic success. It is important to celebrate their achievements and progress in all areas of their education and to support them in setting and achieving their own goals.

In conclusion, supporting academic success in teenagers involves creating a positive learning environment, encouraging effective study habits, providing emotional and practical support, fostering a love of learning, addressing potential barriers, and promoting a healthy lifestyle. It requires a collaborative effort from parents, educators, and caregivers to create an environment that promotes motivation, resilience, and a commitment to learning. By providing the necessary support and resources, encouraging a positive attitude towards education, and recognizing the full scope of academic success, we can help teenagers achieve their academic goals and develop the skills and confidence needed for lifelong learning and success.

❦❦❦

*"Positive relationships are vital for a teenager's well-being. Foster connections based on trust, respect, and open communication. These bonds provide a sense of belonging and support."*

# EIGHT

## PROMOTING HEALTHY FRIENDSHIPS

Promoting healthy friendships is an essential aspect of a teenager's development, contributing significantly to their emotional, social, and psychological well-being. Friendships during adolescence are particularly influential as teenagers seek to establish their identity, gain independence from their families, and navigate the complexities of growing up. Healthy friendships can provide support, boost self-esteem, and teach important life skills, while unhealthy relationships can lead to stress, low self-esteem, and negative behaviors. Therefore, it is crucial to understand the dynamics of teenage friendships and to foster an environment that encourages positive, supportive relationships.

One of the first steps in promoting healthy friendships is helping teenagers understand the qualities that make a good friend. A healthy friendship is built on mutual respect, trust, empathy, and open communication. These relationships are characterized by a balance of give-and-take, where both friends support each other equally and respect each other's boundaries. Encouraging teenagers to seek friends who exhibit these qualities can help them form relationships that are beneficial and supportive. It is also important to teach them to be good friends themselves by showing respect, being trustworthy, practicing empathy, and communicating openly.

Parents and caregivers play a crucial role in modeling healthy relationship behaviors. Teenagers often learn by observing the interactions of adults in their lives. Demonstrating respectful, supportive, and communicative relationships within the family and with others can provide teenagers with a blueprint for their own friendships. It is important for parents to show how to handle conflicts constructively, how to express feelings and needs clearly, and how to offer and receive support. By setting a positive example, parents can help teenagers develop the skills needed to build and maintain healthy friendships.

Encouraging open communication about friendships is also important. Teenagers should feel comfortable discussing their social lives with their parents or caregivers. This includes sharing their experiences, both positive and negative, and seeking advice when needed. Creating a non-judgmental and supportive environment for these conversations can help teenagers feel understood and supported. It is important to listen actively and empathetically, offering guidance without being overly critical or dismissive. Asking open-ended questions can encourage teenagers to reflect on their friendships and consider whether they are healthy and fulfilling. For example, asking questions like "How do you feel when you spend time with this friend?" or "Do you feel supported and respected in this friendship?" can help teenagers evaluate their relationships.

Helping teenagers develop strong social skills is another key aspect of promoting healthy friendships. Social skills such as effective communication, active listening, empathy, and conflict resolution are essential for building and maintaining positive relationships.

These skills can be developed through practice and guidance. Role-playing different social scenarios, discussing strategies for handling conflicts, and encouraging teenagers to express their feelings and needs clearly can all help them develop these important skills. It is also beneficial to provide opportunities for teenagers to practice these skills in real-life settings, such as through group activities, clubs, or team sports.

Encouraging teenagers to participate in extracurricular activities can also help them form healthy friendships. Activities such as sports teams, clubs, volunteer work, or arts programs provide opportunities for teenagers to meet peers with similar interests and values. These settings often promote teamwork, cooperation, and mutual support, which are important components of healthy friendships. Participation in extracurricular activities can also boost self-esteem and provide a sense of belonging, which can contribute to overall well-being. Supporting teenagers in exploring their interests and getting involved in activities they enjoy can help them form positive, lasting friendships.

It is important to discuss and set boundaries around friendships and social interactions. Helping teenagers understand the importance of setting and respecting boundaries can prevent unhealthy dynamics in friendships. This includes teaching them to recognize and assert their own boundaries and to respect the boundaries of others. For example, discussing topics such as personal space, time management, and emotional boundaries can help teenagers navigate their social interactions more effectively. Encouraging them to communicate their boundaries clearly and assertively can empower them to maintain healthy relationships.

Recognizing and addressing unhealthy friendships is also crucial. Unhealthy friendships can involve behaviors such as manipulation, control, disrespect, or exclusion. These relationships can negatively impact a teenager's self-esteem and well-being. It is important for parents and caregivers to be aware of the signs of unhealthy friendships and to discuss these with their teenagers. Encouraging teenagers to reflect on how they feel in their friendships and to trust their instincts if something feels wrong can help them recognize unhealthy dynamics. Providing support and guidance on how to address these situations, such as setting boundaries, seeking support from other friends or adults, or ending the friendship if necessary, can help teenagers navigate these challenges.

Building resilience is another important aspect of promoting healthy friendships. Friendships, like all relationships, can sometimes involve conflicts and challenges. Teaching teenagers how to cope with these situations in a healthy and constructive way can help them maintain positive relationships. This includes developing problem-solving skills, managing stress and emotions, and seeking support when needed. Encouraging teenagers to view conflicts as opportunities for growth and learning rather than as failures can help them develop resilience and a positive mindset.

Supporting teenagers in developing a strong sense of self can also contribute to healthy friendships. When teenagers have a positive self-image and a strong sense of their own values and beliefs, they are better equipped to form relationships that align with their values and support their well-being. Encouraging teenagers to pursue their interests, set personal goals, and build self-confidence can help them develop a strong sense of self. This, in turn, can help them attract and maintain healthy, supportive friendships.

Parents and caregivers can also play a role in fostering a positive peer environment. This can involve hosting social events, encouraging inclusive behavior, and promoting a culture of respect and kindness. Creating opportunities for teenagers to socialize in a safe and supportive environment can help them build positive relationships. Additionally, discussing the importance of kindness, empathy, and respect in social interactions can reinforce these values.

Technology and social media are significant aspects of modern teenage friendships. While these platforms can provide opportunities for connection and communication, they can also present challenges such as cyberbullying, social comparison, and the pressure to maintain a certain online image. It is important for parents and caregivers to discuss the responsible use of technology and social media with their teenagers. This includes setting boundaries around screen time, discussing the potential risks and benefits of social media, and encouraging healthy online behavior. Helping teenagers develop digital literacy skills, such as recognizing cyberbullying and understanding privacy settings, can also promote safe and healthy online interactions.

Finally, fostering a supportive community can contribute to promoting healthy friendships. Encouraging teenagers to build connections with peers, mentors, and other supportive adults can provide them with a network of support. This community can offer guidance, encouragement, and a sense of belonging, which are important for overall well-being. Supporting teenagers in building a strong support network can help them navigate the challenges of adolescence and form positive, lasting friendships.

In conclusion, promoting healthy friendships in teenagers involves understanding the qualities of a good friend, modeling positive relationship behaviors, encouraging open communication, developing social skills, participating in extracurricular activities, setting and respecting boundaries, recognizing and addressing unhealthy friendships, building resilience, supporting a strong sense of self, fostering a positive peer environment, managing technology and social media use, and building a supportive community. By focusing on these aspects, parents, educators, and caregivers can help teenagers develop the skills and confidence needed to form and maintain healthy, supportive friendships. These relationships can provide valuable support, boost self-esteem, and contribute to the overall well-being and development of teenagers.

❦❦❦

"Technology can be a powerful tool for learning, but it also requires responsible use. Teach teenagers to navigate the digital world with caution and integrity. Balance screen time with real-world interactions."

# NINE

# NAVIGATING SOCIAL MEDIA AND TECHNOLOGY

Navigating social media and technology is a critical aspect of modern adolescence. The digital age presents both opportunities and challenges for teenagers as they integrate technology into their daily lives. Social media platforms, smartphones, and the internet offer unprecedented access to information, communication, and entertainment, but they also introduce risks such as cyberbullying, social comparison, and privacy concerns. Supporting teenagers in navigating social media and technology responsibly involves fostering digital literacy, promoting healthy online behavior, setting boundaries, and providing guidance on managing the psychological impacts of digital life.

Understanding the landscape of social media and technology is the first step in helping teenagers navigate it effectively. Social media platforms like Instagram, TikTok, Snapchat, and Twitter play a significant role in teenagers' social lives, offering a space to connect with friends, share experiences, and explore interests. These platforms can enhance social interaction and provide a sense of community. However, they also come with potential downsides, such as exposure to inappropriate content, online harassment, and the pressure to present a curated, idealized version of oneself. Recognizing the dual nature of social media helps parents and caregivers address both the benefits and the risks involved.

Promoting digital literacy is essential for teenagers to navigate the digital world safely and effectively. Digital literacy involves understanding how technology works, recognizing credible sources of information, and knowing how to use digital tools responsibly. Encouraging teenagers to think critically about the content they encounter online is crucial. This includes questioning the accuracy of information, recognizing bias, and understanding the difference between fact and opinion. Teaching teenagers how to evaluate the credibility of sources, cross-check information, and avoid misinformation can help them become more discerning digital consumers.

Healthy online behavior is another key aspect of navigating social media and technology. Encouraging teenagers to engage in positive, respectful interactions online helps create a safer digital environment. This involves teaching them the importance of kindness, empathy, and respect in their digital communications. It is important to discuss the impact of cyberbullying and online harassment and to emphasize the importance of treating others with respect, both online and offline. Encouraging teenagers to think before they post, consider the potential consequences of their actions, and avoid sharing personal or sensitive information can help them navigate social media more safely.

Setting boundaries around technology use is crucial for promoting a balanced and healthy lifestyle. Establishing guidelines for screen time, device usage, and online activities can help teenagers develop healthy habits. This might involve setting specific times for homework, family activities, and sleep, and designating tech-free zones or times, such as during meals or before bedtime. Encouraging teenagers to take regular breaks from screens, engage in physical activities, and spend time outdoors can help prevent the negative effects of excessive screen time, such as eye strain, sleep disturbances, and reduced physical fitness.

Privacy and security are critical considerations when navigating social media and technology. Teenagers need to understand the importance of protecting their personal information and being aware of the privacy settings on the platforms they use. Discussing the potential risks of sharing too much information online, such as identity theft, cyberstalking, and other forms of exploitation, can help teenagers make informed decisions about their online presence. Teaching them how to use strong passwords, enable two-factor authentication, and recognize phishing attempts and other online scams can enhance their digital security.

The psychological impacts of social media and technology are significant and should not be overlooked. Social media can contribute to issues such as anxiety, depression, and low self-esteem, particularly when teenagers engage in social comparison or experience online harassment. It is important to discuss the potential emotional effects of social media use and to encourage teenagers to seek support if they experience negative feelings or situations online. Promoting a healthy self-image and resilience can help teenagers navigate the emotional challenges of the digital world. Encouraging them to focus on their strengths, set realistic goals, and practice self-compassion can counteract the negative impacts of social comparison.

Open communication between parents, caregivers, and teenagers is essential for navigating social media and technology effectively. Creating an environment where teenagers feel comfortable discussing their online experiences, asking questions, and seeking advice can help them make safer and more informed choices. It is important for parents and caregivers to stay informed about the platforms and technologies their teenagers are using and to engage in ongoing conversations about their online activities. This might involve discussing the latest trends, sharing insights about digital safety, and exploring how technology can be used positively.

Role modeling positive technology use is another important strategy for supporting teenagers in navigating social media and technology. Parents and caregivers can set an example by demonstrating balanced and responsible technology use in their own lives. This includes being mindful of screen time, prioritizing face-to-face interactions, and using technology in ways that enhance rather than detract from their well-being. By modeling healthy behaviors, adults can provide a positive framework for teenagers to emulate.

Encouraging teenagers to explore the creative and educational potential of technology can also enhance their digital experience. Technology offers numerous opportunities for learning, creativity, and personal growth. Encouraging teenagers to use digital tools for educational purposes, such as researching topics of interest, participating in online courses, or developing new skills, can help them harness the positive aspects of technology. Additionally, promoting creative activities, such as digital art, video production, or coding, can provide a constructive outlet for their talents and interests.

Supporting teenagers in managing the social dynamics of online interactions is also important. Social media can sometimes amplify social pressures and conflicts, making it challenging for teenagers to navigate their relationships. Helping them develop strategies for managing online interactions, such as setting boundaries with friends, handling disagreements constructively, and seeking help when needed, can reduce the stress associated with digital socialization. Encouraging them to maintain a healthy balance between online and offline interactions can also help them build strong, supportive relationships.

Awareness of the impact of technology on sleep is another critical consideration. The blue light emitted by screens can interfere with the production of melatonin, a hormone that regulates sleep. Encouraging teenagers to limit screen time before bed and to create a relaxing bedtime routine can help improve their sleep quality. Discussing the importance of sleep for overall health and academic performance can motivate teenagers to adopt healthier nighttime habits.

Addressing the addictive potential of technology is another important aspect of supporting teenagers. Social media platforms and digital games are designed to capture and hold users' attention, which can lead to compulsive use. Discussing the signs of technology addiction, such as neglecting responsibilities, withdrawing from offline activities, and experiencing distress when unable to access technology, can help teenagers recognize and address problematic behaviors. Encouraging them to develop a diverse range of interests and activities can reduce their reliance on digital entertainment and promote a more balanced lifestyle.

Providing resources and support for mental health is crucial for helping teenagers navigate the challenges of social media and technology. Access to counseling services, support groups, and educational materials can help teenagers cope with the emotional and psychological impacts of their digital experiences. Encouraging them to seek help when needed and normalizing conversations about mental health can reduce stigma and promote well-being.

Educators also play a significant role in supporting teenagers in navigating social media and technology. Integrating digital literacy education into the curriculum can equip students with the skills and knowledge they need to use technology responsibly. This might involve teaching students about online privacy, digital citizenship, and the ethical use of technology. Providing opportunities for students to discuss their online experiences and learn from one another can also enhance their understanding and resilience.

Community involvement is another important aspect of promoting healthy technology use. Community organizations, such as libraries, youth centers, and advocacy groups, can provide valuable resources and support for teenagers and their families. Workshops, seminars, and informational campaigns can raise awareness about the benefits and risks of social media and technology, and offer practical tips for navigating the digital world. Encouraging community engagement and collaboration can create a supportive network that helps teenagers use technology in positive and empowering ways.

In conclusion, navigating social media and technology is a complex but essential aspect of modern adolescence. Supporting teenagers in this endeavor involves fostering digital literacy, promoting healthy online behavior, setting boundaries, addressing privacy and security concerns, and managing the psychological impacts of digital life. Open communication, positive role modeling, and providing resources and support are key strategies for helping teenagers use technology responsibly and constructively. By working together, parents, caregivers, educators, and communities can create an environment that empowers teenagers to navigate the digital world safely, confidently, and positively. This holistic approach ensures that teenagers can enjoy the benefits of technology while minimizing the associated risks, ultimately contributing to their overall well-being and development.

ᗡᗡᗡ

"Mental health is as important as physical health. Create an environment where teenagers feel safe discussing their feelings. Support them in seeking help when needed."

# TEN

# FOSTERING SELF-ESTEEM AND CONFIDENCE

Fostering self-esteem and confidence in teenagers is a critical aspect of their development, significantly impacting their emotional well-being, academic performance, and social interactions. Self-esteem refers to the overall sense of value and self-worth, while confidence is the belief in one's abilities and potential to achieve goals. These qualities are interrelated and contribute to a teenager's ability to navigate the challenges of adolescence and beyond. To foster self-esteem and confidence, it is essential to create a supportive environment, provide opportunities for success, and teach teenagers to value themselves and their abilities.

Creating a supportive and nurturing environment is the foundation for building self-esteem and confidence in teenagers. This involves showing unconditional love and acceptance, demonstrating that their worth is not contingent on their achievements or behavior. It is important to provide a safe space where teenagers feel valued and understood, allowing them to express their thoughts and emotions freely. Active listening and empathy are key components of this supportive environment, as they help teenagers feel heard and validated. Encouraging open communication and being available to offer guidance and support can significantly impact their sense of self-worth.

Recognizing and celebrating achievements, both big and small, is crucial in fostering self-esteem and confidence. Acknowledging their efforts and successes, whether it is in academics, sports, arts, or personal projects, reinforces the belief that they are capable and competent. It is important to focus not only on the outcomes but also on the effort and persistence they demonstrate. Praising their hard work, determination, and resilience helps them understand that these qualities are valuable and contribute to their success. This approach encourages a growth mindset, where they see challenges as opportunities for learning and growth rather than as threats to their self-worth.

Providing opportunities for teenagers to succeed is another vital aspect of building self-esteem and confidence. Encouraging them to set realistic and achievable goals and supporting them in their efforts to reach these goals can help them build a sense of accomplishment. It is important to guide them in breaking down larger goals into smaller, manageable steps, making the process less overwhelming and more attainable. Providing constructive feedback and celebrating their progress along the way can boost their confidence and motivation. Additionally, allowing them to take on responsibilities and make decisions in areas of their lives fosters a sense of autonomy and competence.

Teaching teenagers to value themselves and their abilities involves helping them recognize their unique strengths and qualities. Encouraging self-reflection and self-awareness can help them identify their talents, skills, and areas of interest. This process can be facilitated through activities such as journaling, engaging in hobbies, or participating in activities that allow them to explore their passions. It is important to support them in pursuing their interests and developing their talents, as this can lead to a greater sense of purpose and fulfillment. Helping them understand that their worth is not solely based on external achievements but also on their inherent qualities and character is crucial for building lasting self-esteem.

Challenging negative self-talk and limiting beliefs is another important aspect of fostering self-esteem and confidence. Teenagers often internalize negative messages from their environment, such as criticism from peers, societal pressures, or unrealistic standards portrayed in the media. These negative messages can lead to self-doubt and a diminished sense of self-worth. Teaching teenagers to recognize and challenge these negative thoughts and replace them with positive, affirming statements can help them build a more positive self-image. Encouraging them to practice self-compassion and treat themselves with kindness and understanding, especially in moments of failure or difficulty, can also strengthen their self-esteem.

Building resilience is a key component of fostering self-esteem and confidence. Resilience is the ability to bounce back from setbacks and challenges, and it is essential for maintaining a positive self-image in the face of adversity. Teaching teenagers coping strategies, such as problem-solving skills, stress management techniques, and emotional regulation, can help them navigate difficulties more effectively. Encouraging them to view setbacks as temporary and solvable, rather than as reflections of their worth, can foster a sense of resilience and confidence. Providing a supportive environment where they feel safe to take risks and learn from their mistakes can also contribute to building resilience.

Developing a strong support network is crucial for fostering self-esteem and confidence. Positive relationships with family, friends, teachers, and mentors can provide valuable encouragement, guidance, and affirmation. Encouraging teenagers to build and maintain healthy relationships, and to seek support when needed, can help them feel connected and valued. Being part of a supportive community can also provide opportunities for positive social interactions and experiences that contribute to their sense of belonging and self-worth.

Promoting a healthy lifestyle is another important aspect of fostering self-esteem and confidence. Physical health and well-being are closely linked to emotional and psychological health. Encouraging teenagers to engage in regular physical activity, maintain a balanced diet, and get adequate sleep can have a positive impact on their mood, energy levels, and overall well-being. Teaching them to prioritize self-care and make healthy choices can help them feel more in control of their lives and more confident in their ability to take care of themselves.

Encouraging a balanced perspective on achievement and success is crucial for fostering self-esteem and confidence. It is important to help teenagers understand that success is not solely defined by external achievements, such as grades or awards, but also by personal growth, effort, and the development of character. Encouraging them to set intrinsic goals, such as improving a skill or developing a positive habit, can help them focus on personal growth rather than external validation. This balanced perspective can reduce the pressure to meet unrealistic standards and help them appreciate their unique journey and progress.

Media literacy is also important in fostering self-esteem and confidence in the digital age. Teenagers are constantly exposed to images and messages that can impact their self-perception, such as unrealistic beauty standards, materialism, and the portrayal of idealized lifestyles on social media. Teaching them to critically evaluate media messages and understand the difference between reality and the often curated, edited content they see online can help them maintain a healthy self-image. Encouraging them to curate their digital environment by following positive, uplifting accounts and setting boundaries around social media use can also support their self-esteem.

Finally, fostering self-esteem and confidence involves encouraging teenagers to contribute to their community and make a positive impact. Volunteering, participating in community service, or engaging in acts of kindness can help them develop a sense of purpose and fulfillment. These experiences can reinforce the belief that they have the ability to make a difference and contribute to the well-being of others. Encouraging them to find ways to give back and support their community can help them build a positive self-identity and strengthen their self-esteem.

In conclusion, fostering self-esteem and confidence in teenagers is a multifaceted process that involves creating a supportive environment, recognizing and celebrating achievements, providing opportunities for success, teaching them to value themselves and their abilities, challenging negative self-talk, building resilience, developing a strong support network, promoting a healthy lifestyle, encouraging a balanced perspective on achievement, teaching media literacy, and encouraging community involvement. By focusing on these aspects, parents, educators, and caregivers can help teenagers develop the self-esteem and confidence needed to navigate the challenges of adolescence and build a positive foundation for their future.

ppp

*"Creativity is a powerful outlet for self-expression. Encourage teenagers to explore their passions through art, music, writing, or other creative pursuits. This exploration fosters confidence and self-discovery."*

# ELEVEN

## UNDERSTANDING TEEN MENTAL HEALTH

Understanding teen mental health is essential for fostering their well-being and development. Adolescence is a period of significant physical, emotional, and psychological change. These changes can be both exciting and challenging, and they can impact a teenager's mental health in various ways. To support teens effectively, it is crucial to understand the common mental health issues they may face, the factors that contribute to these issues, and the strategies that can promote mental health and resilience.

Teenagers are susceptible to a range of mental health issues, including anxiety, depression, stress, and eating disorders. Anxiety disorders are among the most common, manifesting as excessive worry, fear, or nervousness that can interfere with daily activities. Symptoms may include restlessness, difficulty concentrating, irritability, and physical symptoms like headaches or stomachaches. Depression, another prevalent issue, involves persistent feelings of sadness, hopelessness, and a loss of interest in activities once enjoyed. It can also lead to changes in appetite, sleep patterns, and energy levels. Stress is a normal part of life, but chronic stress can negatively impact a teenager's mental and physical health, leading to problems such as headaches, sleep disturbances, and weakened immune function. Eating disorders, including anorexia nervosa, bulimia nervosa, and binge-eating disorder, involve unhealthy eating behaviors and an intense focus on body weight and shape. These disorders can have severe physical and psychological consequences.

Several factors contribute to the mental health issues experienced by teenagers. Biological factors, such as genetic predisposition and hormonal changes, can play a significant role. If there is a family history of mental health disorders, a teenager may be at higher risk. The hormonal fluctuations that occur during puberty can also contribute to mood swings and emotional instability. Environmental factors, including family dynamics, peer relationships, and school pressures, significantly impact teen mental health. A supportive, stable home environment can provide a protective buffer, while a dysfunctional or abusive household can exacerbate mental health issues. Peer relationships are critical during adolescence, and positive friendships can offer emotional support and a sense of belonging. Conversely, bullying, peer pressure, and social exclusion can lead to anxiety, depression, and low self-esteem. Academic pressures and the drive to succeed can also contribute to stress and anxiety. The competitive nature of school environments and the fear of failure or disappointing others can create a significant burden for many teenagers.

Social media and technology use is another important factor influencing teen mental health. While social media can offer opportunities for connection and self-expression, it can also contribute to feelings of inadequacy, anxiety, and depression. The constant comparison to others, cyberbullying, and the pressure to maintain a certain online image can be overwhelming. Teenagers may also experience FOMO (fear of missing out), which can lead to anxiety and stress. Additionally, excessive screen time can interfere with sleep, physical activity, and face-to-face interactions, all of which are important for mental health.

Recognizing the signs of mental health issues in teenagers is crucial for early intervention and support. Changes in behavior, mood, and functioning can indicate that a teenager is struggling. These changes might include withdrawal from friends and family, a decline in academic performance, loss of interest in activities, changes in eating and sleeping habits, and increased irritability or aggression. Physical symptoms, such as frequent headaches or stomachaches, can also be a sign of underlying mental health issues. If a teenager expresses feelings of hopelessness, talks about self-harm or suicide, or engages in risky behaviors, it is essential to seek professional help immediately.

Supporting teen mental health involves creating a supportive environment, promoting healthy habits, and providing access to resources and professional help when needed. Building a supportive environment starts with open communication. Encouraging teenagers to talk about their feelings and experiences and actively listening to them without judgment can make a significant difference. It is important to validate their emotions and let them know that it is okay to feel the way they do. Providing a safe, non-judgmental space for them to express themselves can help them feel understood and supported.

Promoting healthy habits is also crucial for mental health. Regular physical activity, a balanced diet, and adequate sleep are foundational for well-being. Exercise has been shown to reduce symptoms of anxiety and depression, improve mood, and boost self-esteem. Encouraging teenagers to engage in physical activities they enjoy, whether it's sports, dancing, or simply going for a walk, can have positive effects on their mental health. A nutritious diet that includes a variety of fruits, vegetables, whole grains, and lean proteins supports overall health and can impact mood and energy levels. Ensuring that teenagers get enough sleep is essential, as sleep deprivation can exacerbate mental health issues. Creating a regular sleep routine and minimizing screen time before bed can help improve sleep quality.

Encouraging mindfulness and stress management techniques can also benefit teen mental health. Mindfulness practices, such as meditation, deep breathing, and yoga, can help teenagers manage stress and anxiety. Teaching them how to recognize and respond to their thoughts and feelings in a non-judgmental way can improve emotional regulation and resilience. Stress management techniques, such as time management skills, prioritizing tasks, and setting realistic goals, can help teenagers cope with academic and social pressures.

Access to resources and professional help is vital for teenagers struggling with mental health issues. School counselors, therapists, and support groups can provide valuable support and guidance. It is important to reduce the stigma associated with seeking help and to encourage teenagers to reach out when they need it. Professional help can include therapy, counseling, and, in some cases, medication. Cognitive-behavioral therapy (CBT) is an effective treatment for anxiety and depression, helping individuals identify and change negative thought patterns and behaviors. Family therapy can also be beneficial, addressing family dynamics and improving communication and support within the family unit.

Educating teenagers about mental health is an important aspect of support. Providing information about common mental health issues, the importance of self-care, and how to seek help can empower them to take charge of their mental well-being. Schools can play a significant role in mental health education, incorporating it into the curriculum and providing resources and support for students. Peer support programs, where trained students offer support and guidance to their peers, can also be effective.

Encouraging social connections and a sense of belonging is crucial for mental health. Positive relationships with family, friends, and the community can provide emotional support and a sense of security. Encouraging teenagers to participate in group activities, clubs, or volunteer work can help them build connections and feel more engaged with their community. Social support can buffer against the negative effects of stress and improve overall well-being.

Helping teenagers develop a strong sense of identity and self-worth is another important aspect of supporting mental health. Encouraging them to explore their interests, set personal goals, and celebrate their achievements can boost self-esteem and confidence. It is important to help them understand that their worth is not determined by external achievements or the opinions of others but by their inherent qualities and values. Teaching them to practice self-compassion and to treat themselves with kindness and understanding can help them build a positive self-image.

In conclusion, understanding teen mental health involves recognizing the common issues they may face, the factors that contribute to these issues, and the strategies that can support their well-being. By creating a supportive environment, promoting healthy habits, providing access to resources and professional help, educating about mental health, encouraging social connections, and helping teenagers develop a strong sense of identity, we can foster their mental health and resilience. Supporting teen mental health is a collective effort that involves parents, caregivers, educators, and the community. Together, we can help teenagers navigate the challenges of adolescence and build a positive foundation for their future well-being.

ppp

"Physical health supports overall well-being.
Promote healthy lifestyle choices such as regular
exercise, balanced nutrition, and adequate sleep.
These habits build a strong foundation for a
healthy life."

# TWELVE
## Encouraging Creative Expression

Encouraging creative expression in teenagers is essential for their overall development and well-being. Creative expression allows teenagers to explore their thoughts, emotions, and identities, providing an outlet for self-discovery and self-expression. It also fosters critical thinking, problem-solving skills, and emotional resilience. Supporting teenagers in their creative endeavors involves providing opportunities, resources, and encouragement to help them explore and develop their unique talents and interests.

Creativity is a fundamental aspect of human nature, and it manifests in various forms, including visual arts, music, writing, dance, theater, and digital media. Each teenager has their own unique way of expressing creativity, and it is important to recognize and nurture these individual differences. By encouraging creative expression, we can help teenagers develop a stronger sense of self and build confidence in their abilities.

One of the most effective ways to encourage creative expression is to provide access to a wide range of creative activities and resources. This can include enrolling teenagers in art classes, music lessons, writing workshops, or theater programs. Schools and community centers often offer extracurricular activities that cater to different creative interests. Providing materials and tools, such as art supplies, musical instruments, or digital software, can also enable teenagers to explore their creativity at home. Creating a dedicated space for creative activities, whether it is a corner of a room or a studio, can provide a conducive environment for artistic exploration.

It is important to encourage experimentation and play in creative pursuits. Creativity often thrives in an environment where there is freedom to explore without fear of judgment or failure. Encouraging teenagers to try new things, experiment with different techniques, and take risks can help them develop their creative skills and discover new passions. It is important to emphasize that the creative process is more important than the final product. By focusing on the joy and exploration involved in creating, rather than the outcome, teenagers can develop a love for creative expression that is not tied to external validation.

Providing positive feedback and constructive criticism is crucial in nurturing creativity. Positive feedback reinforces a teenager's efforts and achievements, boosting their confidence and motivation. Constructive criticism, when delivered in a supportive and respectful manner, can help teenagers improve their skills and learn from their experiences. It is important to balance praise with helpful suggestions, guiding teenagers to reflect on their work and identify areas for growth. Encouraging self-reflection and self-assessment can also help them develop a critical eye and a deeper understanding of their creative process.

Role models and mentors can play a significant role in encouraging creative expression. Exposure to accomplished artists, musicians, writers, and performers can inspire teenagers and provide them with valuable insights into their chosen fields. Mentors can offer guidance, support, and encouragement, helping teenagers navigate the challenges of their creative journeys. Connecting with creative professionals through workshops, masterclasses, or internships can provide teenagers with real-world experience and a deeper understanding of the creative industries.

Encouraging collaboration and community involvement can also enhance creative expression. Working with others on creative projects, such as group art installations, musical ensembles, or theater productions, can foster teamwork, communication, and problem-solving skills. Collaborative projects provide opportunities for teenagers to learn from each other, share ideas, and build supportive relationships. Community involvement, such as participating in local art exhibitions, performances, or festivals, can also provide a platform for teenagers to showcase their work and connect with a broader audience.

Supporting the integration of creative expression into everyday life can make creativity a natural and enjoyable part of a teenager's routine. Encouraging activities such as keeping a journal, sketching, playing an instrument, or engaging in creative writing can help teenagers incorporate creativity into their daily lives. These activities can serve as a form of self-care, providing an outlet for stress relief and emotional expression. Encouraging creative expression in everyday tasks, such as cooking, decorating, or gardening, can also help teenagers see creativity as a versatile and integral part of life.

It is important to recognize and value the cultural and personal significance of creative expression. Creativity is often deeply intertwined with cultural identity and heritage. Encouraging teenagers to explore and celebrate their cultural backgrounds through creative activities can foster a sense of pride and connection to their roots. It is also important to respect and appreciate the diverse ways in which creativity manifests across different cultures and individuals. By celebrating diversity and inclusivity in creative expression, we can create a more enriching and supportive environment for all teenagers.

Technology and digital media offer new and exciting opportunities for creative expression. Digital tools and platforms, such as graphic design software, music production apps, and social media, provide teenagers with innovative ways to create and share their work. Encouraging teenagers to explore digital creativity can help them develop valuable skills that are relevant in today's technology-driven world. It is important to guide them in using these tools responsibly and ethically, emphasizing the importance of originality and respect for intellectual property.

Creativity also plays a vital role in academic and intellectual development. Encouraging creative thinking and problem-solving in academic subjects can enhance learning and engagement. Integrating creative projects into the curriculum, such as science experiments, historical reenactments, or creative writing assignments, can make learning more dynamic and enjoyable. Encouraging teenagers to approach problems with curiosity and an open mind can foster innovation and critical thinking skills that are applicable across all areas of life.

Parents and caregivers can support creative expression by actively participating in creative activities with their teenagers. Engaging in family art projects, attending concerts or theater performances together, or exploring museums and cultural events can create shared experiences and strengthen family bonds. Showing interest in and appreciation for a teenager's creative work, regardless of the medium or level of expertise, reinforces the value of creativity and provides emotional support.

Encouraging creative expression also involves addressing potential barriers and challenges. Teenagers may face obstacles such as lack of resources, fear of failure, or external pressures to conform to certain expectations. It is important to address these challenges with empathy and support. Providing access to affordable or free creative programs, offering emotional encouragement, and advocating for the importance of creativity in education and personal development can help overcome these barriers. It is also important to challenge stereotypes and misconceptions about creativity, emphasizing that it is not limited to artistic talent but is a valuable skill that can be developed and applied in various contexts.

The benefits of encouraging creative expression extend beyond the individual to the broader community and society. Creative expression fosters innovation, cultural enrichment, and social cohesion. By nurturing creativity in teenagers, we contribute to a more vibrant and dynamic society that values and celebrates diverse forms of expression. Creativity also has the potential to drive positive social change, as it encourages new perspectives, empathy, and the exploration of complex issues.

In conclusion, encouraging creative expression in teenagers is a multifaceted endeavor that involves providing opportunities, resources, and support to help them explore and develop their unique talents and interests. By creating a supportive environment, offering positive feedback, connecting with mentors, promoting collaboration and community involvement, integrating creativity into daily life, embracing cultural diversity, leveraging technology, fostering academic creativity, and addressing barriers, we can help teenagers build confidence, develop critical skills, and find joy and fulfillment in their creative pursuits. Supporting creative expression not only benefits individual teenagers but also enriches our communities and society as a whole.

ppp

"Academic and career planning are crucial for future success. Help teenagers set realistic goals and explore their interests. Provide guidance and opportunities for growth."

# THIRTEEN

# Instilling Responsibility and Accountability

Instilling responsibility and accountability in teenagers is a crucial aspect of their development into well-rounded and capable adults. Responsibility involves understanding and accepting the duties and tasks required of one, while accountability means owning up to the consequences of one's actions and decisions. These qualities are essential for success in both personal and professional life. By fostering responsibility and accountability, we help teenagers develop a sense of self-discipline, integrity, and reliability, which are foundational for their future success and well-being.

One of the fundamental steps in instilling responsibility is providing teenagers with age-appropriate tasks and duties. These responsibilities can range from household chores to academic commitments and extracurricular activities. Assigning specific tasks, such as cleaning their room, doing laundry, or helping with meal preparation, helps teenagers understand the importance of contributing to the household. It also teaches them essential life skills that they will need as they transition to adulthood. Consistently assigning and expecting completion of these tasks reinforces the idea that they are accountable for their contributions.

Encouraging teenagers to manage their own schedules and commitments is another important aspect of fostering responsibility. This involves teaching them how to use calendars, planners, or digital tools to keep track of their activities, deadlines, and appointments. By allowing them to take charge of their schedules, teenagers learn to prioritize tasks, manage their time effectively, and balance their various responsibilities. It is important to provide guidance and support as they develop these skills, offering tips on time management and organization while allowing them the autonomy to make their own decisions and learn from their experiences.

Academic responsibilities are a significant part of a teenager's life. Encouraging them to take ownership of their education by setting goals, managing their assignments, and seeking help when needed promotes a sense of accountability for their learning. It is important to foster a growth mindset, where effort and persistence are valued over innate ability. By emphasizing the importance of hard work and the process of learning, rather than just the final grades, teenagers can develop a more resilient and motivated approach to their education. Providing a supportive environment where they feel comfortable asking for help and discussing their challenges can further reinforce their sense of responsibility for their academic success.

Extracurricular activities and part-time jobs also offer valuable opportunities for teenagers to develop responsibility and accountability. Participation in sports, clubs, or volunteer work requires commitment, teamwork, and reliability. These activities teach teenagers to follow through on their commitments, work collaboratively with others, and manage their time effectively. Part-time jobs, in particular, can provide practical experience in handling responsibilities such as showing up on time, completing tasks efficiently, and managing finances. These experiences help teenagers understand the expectations of the workplace and develop skills that will be essential in their future careers.

Open communication and clear expectations are vital in fostering responsibility and accountability. Teenagers need to understand what is expected of them and why these expectations are important. Clear communication about rules, responsibilities, and the consequences of not meeting them helps teenagers understand the impact of their actions. It is important to involve them in discussions about family rules and expectations, allowing them to express their opinions and negotiate agreements. This collaborative approach fosters a sense of ownership and accountability, as teenagers are more likely to adhere to rules and responsibilities that they have helped establish.

Consequences, both positive and negative, play a crucial role in teaching accountability. Positive reinforcement, such as praise or rewards for completing tasks and meeting expectations, can motivate teenagers to take responsibility for their actions. It is important to acknowledge their efforts and successes, reinforcing the idea that responsible behavior is valued and appreciated. Negative consequences, such as losing privileges or facing additional tasks, should be used to address failures to meet responsibilities. It is important to ensure that consequences are fair, consistent, and directly related to the behavior in question. This helps teenagers understand the connection between their actions and the outcomes, reinforcing their sense of accountability.

Modeling responsible and accountable behavior is one of the most effective ways to teach these qualities. Teenagers often learn by observing the adults in their lives. Demonstrating reliability, honesty, and integrity in your own actions sets a powerful example for them to follow. This includes fulfilling your own responsibilities, admitting mistakes, and taking corrective action when necessary. Discussing your decision-making processes and explaining how you handle your own responsibilities can provide valuable insights and guidance for teenagers. By modeling responsible behavior, you show teenagers that these qualities are important and achievable.

Encouraging self-reflection and self-assessment helps teenagers develop a deeper understanding of responsibility and accountability. Regularly discussing their experiences, challenges, and successes allows them to reflect on their actions and identify areas for improvement. Encouraging them to set personal goals and track their progress fosters a sense of ownership over their development. It is important to create a supportive environment where they feel comfortable discussing their mistakes and learning from them. By promoting self-reflection, you help teenagers develop the ability to evaluate their own behavior and make responsible decisions.

Teaching decision-making skills is another crucial aspect of instilling responsibility and accountability. Helping teenagers understand the steps involved in making thoughtful and informed decisions can empower them to take control of their actions. This includes identifying the problem, considering different options, weighing the potential consequences, and making a choice. Encouraging them to think critically about their decisions and to consider the long-term effects can help them develop a more responsible approach to problem-solving. Providing opportunities for them to practice decision-making, both in low-stakes and more significant situations, helps build their confidence and competence in this area.

Building resilience and coping skills is essential for helping teenagers handle the challenges and setbacks they will inevitably face. Teaching them how to manage stress, handle disappointment, and recover from mistakes fosters a sense of accountability for their emotional well-being. Encouraging them to develop healthy coping strategies, such as exercise, mindfulness, or talking to a trusted friend or adult, can help them navigate difficult situations more effectively. By building resilience, teenagers are better equipped to take responsibility for their actions and learn from their experiences.

Encouraging community involvement and social responsibility can also help teenagers develop a broader sense of accountability. Participating in community service, volunteering, or engaging in civic activities teaches them the importance of contributing to the well-being of others and the community. These experiences help them understand the impact of their actions on a larger scale and foster a sense of responsibility for making positive contributions to society. Encouraging them to take on leadership roles in these activities can further develop their sense of accountability and their ability to take initiative.

Fostering a positive self-image and self-worth is important for developing responsibility and accountability. Teenagers who feel confident in their abilities and value themselves are more likely to take ownership of their actions and strive to meet their responsibilities. Encouraging them to recognize their strengths, celebrate their achievements, and set realistic goals can help build their self-esteem. It is important to provide support and encouragement, while also challenging them to push their boundaries and take on new responsibilities. By fostering a positive self-image, you help teenagers develop the confidence and motivation needed to take responsibility for their actions.

Providing opportunities for independence and autonomy is crucial for developing responsibility and accountability. Allowing teenagers to make their own choices, take on challenges, and learn from their mistakes fosters a sense of ownership over their lives. It is important to strike a balance between providing guidance and support, and allowing them the freedom to explore and take risks. Encouraging them to take on new responsibilities, such as managing their own finances, making decisions about their education and career, or planning and organizing events, helps them develop the skills and confidence needed to navigate adulthood.

In conclusion, instilling responsibility and accountability in teenagers is a multifaceted process that involves providing opportunities, setting clear expectations, modeling responsible behavior, and encouraging self-reflection and decision-making. By fostering a supportive environment, promoting positive reinforcement and fair consequences, and encouraging independence and community involvement, we can help teenagers develop the qualities needed for success in both personal and professional life. These efforts not only contribute to their growth and development but also prepare them to become responsible, accountable, and capable adults who can navigate the complexities of the world with confidence and integrity.

ppp

"Failure is not a setback, but a stepping stone to success. Teach teenagers to view challenges as opportunities for learning. Encourage resilience and perseverance."

# FOURTEEN

## HEALTHY LIFESTYLE CHOICES

Adopting healthy lifestyle choices during adolescence is crucial for ensuring long-term well-being and preventing future health issues. Teenagers are at a stage where they are developing habits that will likely follow them into adulthood, making it essential to guide them in making positive choices regarding nutrition, physical activity, sleep, and mental health. A healthy lifestyle supports physical development, mental well-being, and academic success, and lays the foundation for a fulfilling life.

Nutrition plays a vital role in maintaining good health. During adolescence, the body undergoes significant growth and changes, increasing the need for nutrients. A balanced diet that includes a variety of fruits, vegetables, whole grains, lean proteins, and healthy fats is essential for supporting this growth and providing energy. Encouraging teenagers to eat regular, balanced meals and to make healthy snack choices helps them maintain stable energy levels and concentration. It is important to educate them about the benefits of different food groups and how they contribute to their health. For example, calcium-rich foods like dairy products and leafy greens are crucial for bone development, while proteins support muscle growth and repair. Guiding teenagers to limit their intake of processed foods, sugary drinks, and excessive fats can help prevent health issues such as obesity, diabetes, and cardiovascular diseases. Promoting the habit of reading food labels and understanding nutritional information empowers them to make informed choices about what they consume.

Physical activity is another cornerstone of a healthy lifestyle. Regular exercise is essential for maintaining a healthy weight, building strong muscles and bones, and promoting cardiovascular health. It also has mental health benefits, such as reducing symptoms of anxiety and depression, improving mood, and enhancing cognitive function. Encouraging teenagers to find physical activities they enjoy can increase their likelihood of staying active. This can include team sports, individual sports, dance, martial arts, or even activities like hiking or cycling. Schools and communities can support this by providing access to sports facilities, clubs, and events that promote physical activity. It is recommended that teenagers engage in at least 60 minutes of moderate to vigorous physical activity each day. This can be broken up into shorter periods throughout the day, making it more manageable and enjoyable. Encouraging a mix of aerobic activities, strength training, and flexibility exercises can provide comprehensive health benefits.

Sleep is a critical, yet often overlooked, component of a healthy lifestyle. Adequate sleep is essential for physical health, cognitive function, and emotional well-being. Teenagers need about 8 to 10 hours of sleep per night to support their growth and development. However, many teenagers do not get enough sleep due to busy schedules, academic pressures, and the use of electronic devices. Chronic sleep deprivation can lead to issues such as impaired concentration, mood swings, weakened immune function, and increased risk of mental health problems. Establishing a regular sleep routine can help teenagers get the rest they need. Encouraging them to go to bed and wake up at the same time each day, even on weekends, helps regulate their internal clock. Creating a relaxing bedtime routine, such as reading a book, taking a warm bath, or practicing mindfulness, can signal to their body that it is time to wind down. It is also important to limit exposure to screens before bedtime, as the blue light emitted by devices can interfere with the production of melatonin, the hormone that regulates sleep.

Mental health is an integral part of a healthy lifestyle. Adolescence can be a challenging time, with many teenagers experiencing stress, anxiety, and depression. Promoting mental health involves providing support, fostering resilience, and encouraging positive coping strategies. Open communication is key to supporting a teenager's mental health. Creating an environment where they feel comfortable discussing their feelings and concerns can help them feel understood and supported. Encouraging them to engage in activities that promote relaxation and stress relief, such as mindfulness, meditation, yoga, or hobbies they enjoy, can help them manage stress. It is important to recognize the signs of mental health issues and to seek professional help if needed. This can include therapy, counseling, or support groups. Schools and communities can play a significant role by providing resources and programs that promote mental health and well-being.

Building strong social connections is also vital for a healthy lifestyle. Positive relationships with family, friends, and the community provide emotional support, reduce stress, and enhance overall well-being. Encouraging teenagers to build and maintain healthy relationships can help them develop a sense of belonging and self-worth. This can involve participating in group activities, clubs, or volunteer work, which provide opportunities for social interaction and connection. It is important to teach them the value of empathy, communication, and mutual respect in their relationships.

Avoiding harmful behaviors is another critical aspect of a healthy lifestyle. Educating teenagers about the risks associated with substance abuse, smoking, and risky sexual behaviors can help them make informed decisions. Providing accurate information about the consequences of these behaviors and promoting healthy alternatives can reduce their likelihood of engaging in them. Encouraging open and honest discussions about these topics can help teenagers feel more comfortable seeking advice and support if they encounter these issues. It is also important to provide resources and support for those who may already be struggling with these behaviors.

Encouraging teenagers to develop healthy coping mechanisms for dealing with stress and emotions is essential. Life inevitably involves challenges and setbacks, and how they cope with these situations can significantly impact their well-being. Teaching them strategies such as problem-solving, time management, and emotional regulation can help them handle stress more effectively. Encouraging them to engage in physical activity, spend time in nature, practice mindfulness, or talk to a trusted friend or adult can provide healthy outlets for managing stress. It is important to model healthy coping mechanisms and to provide support and encouragement as they develop their own strategies.

Education and awareness are crucial in promoting a healthy lifestyle. Providing teenagers with accurate and relevant information about health and wellness empowers them to make informed decisions. Schools can play a significant role by incorporating health education into the curriculum, covering topics such as nutrition, physical activity, mental health, and substance abuse. Parents and caregivers can also support this by discussing health topics at home and providing guidance and support. Encouraging teenagers to take an active role in their health and well-being helps them develop a sense of responsibility and ownership.

Promoting a healthy lifestyle also involves fostering a positive body image and self-esteem. Adolescence is a time of significant physical changes, and many teenagers may struggle with body image issues. Encouraging a positive self-image involves promoting self-acceptance and helping them appreciate their unique qualities. It is important to challenge societal and media-driven standards of beauty and to emphasize that health and well-being are more important than appearance. Encouraging healthy behaviors for the sake of well-being rather than appearance can help teenagers develop a more positive relationship with their bodies.

Technology and social media can have both positive and negative impacts on a teenager's health. While these tools can provide valuable information, social connections, and entertainment, they can also contribute to issues such as sedentary behavior, sleep disturbances, and mental health concerns. Encouraging teenagers to use technology mindfully and to set boundaries around screen time can help mitigate these negative effects. Promoting a balance between online and offline activities, and encouraging them to engage in physical activities, social interactions, and hobbies outside of the digital world, supports a healthier lifestyle.

Finally, fostering a healthy lifestyle involves creating an environment that supports and encourages healthy choices. This includes providing access to healthy foods, safe spaces for physical activity, and resources for mental health support. It also involves promoting a culture that values health and well-being, both at home and in the community. By setting a positive example and providing support and encouragement, parents, caregivers, educators, and community leaders can help teenagers develop the habits and attitudes needed for a healthy and fulfilling life.

In conclusion, adopting healthy lifestyle choices during adolescence is essential for long-term well-being and development. By promoting balanced nutrition, regular physical activity, adequate sleep, mental health, strong social connections, and avoiding harmful behaviors, we can help teenagers build a foundation for a healthy future. Providing education, support, and a positive environment empowers them to make informed decisions and develop habits that will benefit them throughout their lives. Supporting teenagers in making healthy lifestyle choices not only enhances their current well-being but also sets them on a path to a healthier, more fulfilling adulthood.

ᐯᐯᐯ

"Volunteerism fosters empathy and social responsibility. Encourage teenagers to give back to their communities. These experiences build character and a sense of purpose."

# FIFTEEN

## SEXUALITY AND RELATIONSHIPS

Understanding and navigating sexuality and relationships is a crucial part of adolescence. As teenagers go through physical, emotional, and psychological changes, they begin to explore their sexual identity and form romantic relationships. This period of exploration and discovery is vital for their development, but it also comes with challenges and risks. Providing accurate information, emotional support, and open communication is essential to help teenagers make informed decisions and develop healthy attitudes toward sexuality and relationships.

Sexuality is a natural and integral part of being human. It encompasses sexual orientation, sexual behavior, gender identity, and reproductive health. During adolescence, teenagers become more aware of their sexual feelings and attractions, which can be exciting but also confusing and overwhelming.

It is important to provide comprehensive and accurate sex education that covers a wide range of topics, including anatomy, reproduction, contraception, consent, and sexually transmitted infections (STIs). This education should be age-appropriate and culturally sensitive, providing teenagers with the knowledge they need to make informed decisions about their sexual health.

Open and honest communication about sexuality is essential. Parents and caregivers play a crucial role in providing information and guidance. Creating a safe and non-judgmental environment where teenagers feel comfortable discussing their questions and concerns about sexuality can help them navigate this complex aspect of their lives. It is important to listen actively, validate their feelings, and provide accurate information without shaming or scaring them. Encouraging teenagers to ask questions and seek reliable sources of information can empower them to make informed choices about their sexual health.

Understanding and accepting one's sexual orientation is a significant part of a teenager's development. Sexual orientation refers to the emotional, romantic, and sexual attraction a person feels toward others. This can include heterosexuality, homosexuality, bisexuality, and other orientations. It is important to support teenagers in exploring and understanding their sexual orientation without judgment or pressure. Creating an inclusive and accepting environment, both at home and in the community, helps teenagers feel safe and valued.

This support is especially important for LGBTQ+ teenagers, who may face additional challenges such as discrimination, bullying, and rejection. Providing access to supportive resources, such as LGBTQ+ organizations and counseling services, can help them navigate these challenges and build a positive self-identity.

Gender identity is another critical aspect of sexuality. Gender identity refers to a person's internal sense of being male, female, a blend of both, or neither, and it may or may not align with the sex assigned at birth. Adolescence is a time when many individuals begin to explore and express their gender identity. It is important to respect and support teenagers' exploration of their gender identity, using their chosen names and pronouns and providing a safe space for them to express themselves. Educating oneself about gender diversity and challenging stereotypes and misconceptions can help create a more inclusive and supportive environment.

Romantic relationships are a significant part of adolescent development. These relationships provide opportunities for emotional connection, companionship, and the exploration of intimacy. However, they can also be sources of stress and conflict. It is important to help teenagers understand what constitutes a healthy relationship. Healthy relationships are based on mutual respect, trust, communication, and equality. Encouraging teenagers to reflect on their values and boundaries and to communicate openly with their partners can help them build healthy and fulfilling relationships.

It is also important to discuss the concept of consent, emphasizing that consent must be clear, enthusiastic, and ongoing. Teaching teenagers to respect their own and others' boundaries and to recognize the signs of unhealthy or abusive relationships is crucial for their safety and well-being.

Addressing the emotional aspects of sexuality and relationships is essential. Adolescence is a time of heightened emotions and intense feelings. Teenagers may experience strong romantic and sexual attractions, which can be confusing and overwhelming. It is important to validate their feelings and provide guidance on how to manage these emotions in a healthy way.

Encouraging self-awareness and emotional regulation can help teenagers navigate the complexities of their relationships and sexual experiences. Providing support and reassurance, especially during times of heartbreak or relationship conflict, can help them build resilience and develop a healthy attitude toward relationships.

Contraception and safe sex practices are critical topics in sexual education. Providing accurate information about different methods of contraception, including their effectiveness and potential side effects, helps teenagers make informed decisions about their sexual health. It is important to discuss the use of condoms and other barrier methods to prevent STIs and unintended pregnancies.

Encouraging teenagers to take responsibility for their sexual health and to communicate openly with their partners about contraception and STI prevention is essential. Access to reproductive health services, including confidential consultations and contraceptive options, supports teenagers in making safe and informed choices.

The influence of media and technology on teenagers' understanding of sexuality and relationships cannot be overlooked. Social media, television, movies, and the internet expose teenagers to a wide range of messages about sex and relationships. Some of these messages may be unrealistic, misleading, or harmful. Encouraging media literacy helps teenagers critically evaluate the content they consume and recognize the difference between healthy and unhealthy portrayals of relationships. Discussing the impact of pornography and the importance of consent and mutual respect in real-life sexual encounters is also crucial.

Cultural and societal norms play a significant role in shaping teenagers' attitudes toward sexuality and relationships. These norms can vary widely and may influence beliefs about gender roles, sexual behavior, and relationships. It is important to acknowledge and respect cultural differences while also promoting healthy and respectful attitudes. Encouraging teenagers to question harmful stereotypes and to develop their own values and beliefs about sexuality and relationships can help them make informed and autonomous decisions.

Supporting teenagers in developing a positive body image is also important for their sexual and emotional well-being. Adolescence is a time of significant physical changes, and many teenagers may feel self-conscious or insecure about their bodies. Promoting self-acceptance and challenging societal standards of beauty can help teenagers develop a healthier relationship with their bodies. Encouraging them to focus on their strengths and to appreciate their bodies for their functionality rather than appearance can foster a positive self-image.

Peer influence is another significant factor in teenagers' sexual and relational development. Friends and peers can provide support and guidance, but they can also contribute to pressure and risky behaviors. It is important to help teenagers navigate peer pressure by building their self-confidence and assertiveness. Encouraging them to make decisions based on their own values and boundaries rather than seeking approval from others can help them develop healthier relationships. Providing opportunities for positive peer interactions and role models can also support their development.

Education and support from schools and community organizations play a crucial role in promoting healthy sexuality and relationships. Comprehensive sex education programs that cover a wide range of topics, including consent, communication, contraception, and healthy relationships, provide teenagers with the knowledge and skills they need to make informed decisions. Schools and community organizations can also provide access to resources, such as counseling services, support groups, and health clinics, that support teenagers' sexual and emotional well-being.

In conclusion, understanding and navigating sexuality and relationships is a complex and essential part of adolescence. Providing accurate information, emotional support, and open communication is crucial for helping teenagers make informed decisions and develop healthy attitudes toward sexuality and relationships.

By creating a supportive and inclusive environment, promoting comprehensive sex education, respecting individual differences, and encouraging positive peer interactions, we can help teenagers build the foundation for healthy and fulfilling sexual and relational lives. Supporting teenagers in this journey not only enhances their current well-being but also prepares them for a lifetime of healthy and respectful relationships.

🍂🍂🍂

"A safe and supportive home environment is essential for development. Be present, listen actively, and show unconditional love. This support nurtures confidence and resilience."

# SIXTEEN

# DEALING WITH PEER PRESSURE

Dealing with peer pressure is an inevitable part of adolescence, as teenagers navigate the complexities of social dynamics and strive to establish their identity. Peer pressure can influence behavior, decisions, and attitudes, both positively and negatively. Understanding the mechanisms of peer pressure, recognizing its effects, and developing strategies to cope with it are crucial for helping teenagers make informed and autonomous choices. Providing support, education, and guidance can empower teenagers to resist negative influences and build resilience against peer pressure.

Peer pressure arises from the desire to fit in and be accepted by a group. During adolescence, the importance of peer relationships increases significantly, as teenagers seek to establish their identity and gain independence from their families. This heightened sensitivity to peer approval can lead to conformity and the adoption of behaviors and attitudes that align with the group's norms. Peer pressure can manifest in various forms, including direct pressure, where peers explicitly encourage or coerce an individual to engage in a specific behavior, and indirect pressure, where the individual feels compelled to conform to perceived group norms without explicit prompting.

Positive peer pressure can motivate teenagers to adopt beneficial behaviors, such as studying hard, participating in extracurricular activities, or engaging in community service. However, negative peer pressure can lead to risky behaviors, such as substance abuse, delinquency, and unsafe sexual practices. It is important to help teenagers recognize the difference between positive and negative peer pressure and to understand the potential consequences of their choices.

One of the key strategies for dealing with peer pressure is building self-esteem and confidence. Teenagers with a strong sense of self-worth and confidence in their abilities are more likely to resist negative influences and make decisions based on their own values and beliefs. Encouraging teenagers to pursue their interests, set personal goals, and celebrate their achievements can help build their self-esteem. Providing support and positive reinforcement, while also challenging them to push their boundaries and take on new responsibilities, fosters a sense of competence and self-assurance.

Teaching assertiveness skills is crucial for helping teenagers resist peer pressure. Assertiveness involves expressing one's thoughts, feelings, and needs clearly and confidently without being aggressive or passive. Encouraging teenagers to practice assertive communication, such as using "I" statements and setting clear boundaries, can empower them to stand up for themselves and make their own choices. Role-playing different scenarios and discussing strategies for handling peer pressure can help teenagers develop these skills and feel more prepared to face challenging situations.

Open communication with parents and caregivers is essential for supporting teenagers in dealing with peer pressure. Creating a safe and non-judgmental environment where teenagers feel comfortable discussing their experiences and concerns can help them feel understood and supported. Active listening, empathy, and validation of their feelings are key components of effective communication. Providing guidance and advice, while also respecting their autonomy, helps teenagers navigate peer pressure with confidence. It is important to discuss the potential risks and consequences of succumbing to negative peer pressure and to encourage critical thinking and decision-making.

Helping teenagers develop a strong sense of values and principles can provide a solid foundation for making autonomous choices. Encouraging them to reflect on their beliefs, goals, and what they stand for can help them develop a clear sense of identity and purpose. Discussing ethical and moral dilemmas and exploring different perspectives can enhance their ability to think critically and make informed decisions. When teenagers have a strong sense of their values and principles, they are more likely to resist peer pressure and make choices that align with their beliefs.

Providing opportunities for positive peer interactions and friendships is another important strategy for dealing with peer pressure. Encouraging teenagers to build relationships with peers who share their values and interests can provide a supportive network that reinforces positive behaviors. Participation in group activities, clubs, sports, or volunteer work can help teenagers develop healthy and supportive friendships. These positive relationships can serve as a buffer against negative peer pressure and provide a sense of belonging and acceptance.

Educating teenagers about the tactics used in peer pressure and the potential risks associated with certain behaviors is crucial for their ability to resist negative influences. Providing accurate information about the consequences of substance abuse, risky sexual behavior, and other harmful activities helps teenagers make informed decisions. It is important to emphasize that they have the right to say no and to make choices that are best for their well-being. Discussing real-life examples and sharing stories of individuals who have successfully resisted peer pressure can provide inspiration and practical insights.

Encouraging teenagers to develop problem-solving and coping skills can help them manage the stress and challenges associated with peer pressure. Teaching them strategies for managing stress, such as mindfulness, relaxation techniques, and physical activity, can enhance their emotional resilience. Providing guidance on how to handle conflicts and difficult situations, such as seeking support from trusted adults or peers, can help teenagers feel more equipped to deal with peer pressure. It is important to foster a growth mindset, where teenagers view challenges as opportunities for learning and growth rather than as threats.

Role modeling positive behaviors and attitudes is one of the most effective ways to teach teenagers how to deal with peer pressure. Teenagers often learn by observing the actions and decisions of the adults in their lives. Demonstrating integrity, resilience, and the ability to make autonomous choices sets a powerful example for them to follow. Discussing your own experiences with peer pressure and how you handled challenging situations can provide valuable lessons and insights. By modeling positive behaviors, you show teenagers that it is possible to resist negative influences and stay true to oneself.

Building a supportive community that reinforces positive values and behaviors can also help teenagers deal with peer pressure. Schools, community organizations, and peer groups can play a significant role in promoting healthy behaviors and providing support. Programs that focus on leadership development, character education, and social-emotional learning can enhance teenagers' ability to make positive choices and resist negative peer pressure.

Creating opportunities for teenagers to take on leadership roles and make meaningful contributions to their community can empower them to become role models for their peers.

Encouraging media literacy is another important strategy for helping teenagers deal with peer pressure. Media and technology play a significant role in shaping teenagers' perceptions of social norms and behaviors. Teaching teenagers to critically evaluate the messages they receive from social media, television, movies, and other sources can help them recognize unrealistic and harmful portrayals of behavior. Discussing the influence of advertising, celebrity culture, and peer dynamics in media can enhance their ability to make informed and autonomous choices.

Providing access to resources and support services is crucial for teenagers who are struggling with peer pressure. Counseling services, support groups, and educational programs can provide valuable guidance and assistance. Encouraging teenagers to seek help when needed and normalizing conversations about peer pressure and mental health can reduce stigma and promote well-being. Schools and community organizations can play a significant role in providing resources and support for teenagers and their families.

In conclusion, dealing with peer pressure is a complex and multifaceted challenge for teenagers. Providing support, education, and guidance can empower them to resist negative influences and make informed and autonomous choices. By building self-esteem and confidence, teaching assertiveness skills, fostering open communication, developing a strong sense of values and principles, encouraging positive peer interactions, educating about the risks associated with certain behaviors, promoting problem-solving and coping skills, role modeling positive behaviors, building a supportive community, encouraging media literacy, and providing access to resources and support services, we can help teenagers navigate the complexities of peer pressure and build resilience against negative influences. Supporting teenagers in this journey not only enhances their current well-being but also prepares them for a lifetime of healthy and autonomous decision-making.

ᐅᐅᐅ

"Encouraging self-expression helps teenagers explore their identities. Provide opportunities for them to discover and develop their unique talents. Celebrate their individuality and creativity."

# SEVENTEEN

## PREPARING FOR THE FUTURE

Preparing teenagers for the future is a critical aspect of their development, involving a comprehensive approach that encompasses academic readiness, career planning, life skills, and emotional resilience. This preparation is essential to equip them with the knowledge, skills, and attitudes needed to navigate the complexities of adulthood successfully. The process involves fostering a growth mindset, encouraging self-awareness, and providing practical experiences that help teenagers make informed decisions about their futures.

Academic readiness is a foundational component of preparing teenagers for the future. Ensuring that they have a strong educational background is crucial for their success in higher education and their careers. This involves not only mastering core subjects but also developing critical thinking, problem-solving, and analytical skills. Encouraging a love of learning and intellectual curiosity can help teenagers engage more deeply with their studies and see education as a lifelong endeavor. Providing access to diverse educational resources, such as books, online courses, and tutoring, can enhance their learning experience and help them explore various fields of interest.

Career planning is another essential aspect of future preparation. Helping teenagers understand the range of career options available to them and the pathways to those careers can empower them to make informed choices. This process begins with self-assessment, where teenagers reflect on their interests, strengths, values, and goals. Tools such as personality tests, career assessments, and informational interviews with professionals can provide valuable insights into potential career paths. Encouraging teenagers to explore different careers through internships, job shadowing, and volunteer work can provide practical experience and help them make more informed decisions.

Developing life skills is critical for teenagers to navigate adulthood successfully. These skills include financial literacy, time management, communication, and decision-making. Financial literacy involves understanding how to manage money, create a budget, save for the future, and make informed financial decisions. Teaching teenagers about the importance of saving, investing, and avoiding debt can help them build a strong financial foundation. Time management skills, such as setting priorities, creating schedules, and balancing responsibilities, are essential for academic and professional success. Effective communication skills, including listening, speaking, and writing, are crucial for building relationships and achieving goals. Decision-making skills, which involve evaluating options, considering consequences, and making informed choices, are vital for personal and professional growth.

Emotional resilience is a key factor in preparing teenagers for the future. Life is full of challenges and setbacks, and the ability to cope with adversity is crucial for long-term success and well-being. Building emotional resilience involves fostering a positive mindset, encouraging self-awareness, and teaching coping strategies. Encouraging teenagers to view challenges as opportunities for growth and to learn from their mistakes can help them develop a resilient attitude. Providing support and guidance during difficult times, such as academic pressure or personal conflicts, can help them build coping skills and emotional strength. Techniques such as mindfulness, meditation, and stress management can also enhance emotional resilience.

Social and interpersonal skills are also essential for future success. Building strong relationships, working collaboratively, and understanding different perspectives are important in both personal and professional contexts. Encouraging teenagers to engage in group activities, such as team sports, clubs, or community service, can help them develop these skills. Teaching empathy, respect, and conflict resolution can enhance their ability to navigate social interactions and build positive relationships. Encouraging them to develop a network of supportive peers, mentors, and professionals can provide valuable resources and opportunities for personal and career growth.

Health and well-being are fundamental components of preparing for the future. Encouraging teenagers to adopt healthy lifestyle habits, such as regular exercise, balanced nutrition, and adequate sleep, can support their physical and mental health. Educating them about the importance of self-care and stress management can help them maintain their well-being amidst the demands of adult life. Providing access to resources such as health education, counseling, and wellness programs can support their overall development and resilience.

Technology and digital literacy are increasingly important in today's world. Ensuring that teenagers are proficient in using technology and understanding its implications is crucial for their future success. This involves not only technical skills, such as using software and navigating digital platforms but also understanding the ethical and social implications of technology use. Encouraging teenagers to use technology responsibly, protect their privacy, and understand the impact of their digital footprint can help them navigate the digital world safely and effectively. Providing opportunities for them to learn about emerging technologies, such as artificial intelligence, coding, and digital marketing, can enhance their career prospects and prepare them for the evolving job market.

Encouraging teenagers to set goals and create action plans is another important aspect of future preparation. Goal-setting helps them clarify their aspirations and develop a sense of purpose and direction. Encouraging them to set specific, measurable, achievable, relevant, and time-bound (SMART) goals can enhance their motivation and focus. Teaching them how to create action plans, break goals into manageable steps, and track their progress can help them stay organized and on track. Celebrating their achievements and milestones, no matter how small, can boost their confidence and reinforce their commitment to their goals.

Cultural competence and global awareness are increasingly important in our interconnected world. Encouraging teenagers to learn about different cultures, perspectives, and global issues can enhance their ability to navigate diverse environments and build inclusive relationships. Providing opportunities for cultural exchange, travel, and engagement with global issues can broaden their horizons and deepen their understanding of the world. Teaching them to appreciate diversity, challenge stereotypes, and advocate for social justice can help them become responsible and empathetic global citizens.

Encouraging a growth mindset is fundamental to preparing teenagers for the future. A growth mindset, the belief that abilities and intelligence can be developed through effort and learning, fosters resilience, motivation, and a love of learning. Encouraging teenagers to embrace challenges, persist in the face of setbacks, and view effort as a path to mastery can help them develop a positive and proactive approach to their goals. Providing constructive feedback, celebrating effort and progress, and promoting a culture of learning and improvement can reinforce a growth mindset.

Providing mentorship and guidance is crucial for helping teenagers navigate their future paths. Mentors, whether they are parents, teachers, or professionals, can provide valuable insights, support, and encouragement. Encouraging teenagers to seek out mentors and role models who inspire them can provide guidance and inspiration. Mentorship programs, career counseling, and networking opportunities can also support their development and connect them with resources and opportunities.

Community involvement and civic engagement are important aspects of preparing teenagers for the future. Encouraging them to participate in community service, volunteer work, and civic activities can help them develop a sense of responsibility, empathy, and social awareness. These experiences can also enhance their leadership skills, build their network, and provide valuable insights into social issues and community needs. Teaching them about their rights and responsibilities as citizens and encouraging them to engage in civic activities, such as voting and advocacy, can foster a sense of civic duty and empowerment.

Preparing teenagers for the future also involves fostering creativity and innovation. Encouraging them to think outside the box, explore new ideas, and take creative risks can enhance their problem-solving skills and adaptability. Providing opportunities for creative expression, such as art, music, writing, or entrepreneurship, can help them develop their talents and passions. Encouraging a culture of curiosity, experimentation, and innovation can inspire them to pursue their interests and make meaningful contributions to their fields.

Finally, it is important to foster a sense of agency and autonomy in teenagers. Encouraging them to take ownership of their decisions, actions, and future paths empowers them to become self-reliant and responsible adults. Providing opportunities for them to make choices, take on responsibilities, and learn from their experiences fosters a sense of independence and competence. Encouraging them to advocate for themselves, seek out opportunities, and take initiative helps them develop a proactive and empowered approach to their future.

In conclusion, preparing teenagers for the future is a multifaceted and ongoing process that involves academic readiness, career planning, life skills, emotional resilience, social and interpersonal skills, health and well-being, technology and digital literacy, goal-setting, cultural competence, growth mindset, mentorship, community involvement, creativity, and fostering agency. By providing support, guidance, and opportunities in these areas, we can help teenagers build a strong foundation for their future success and well-being. Empowering them to make informed decisions, pursue their passions, and navigate the complexities of adulthood with confidence and resilience prepares them for a fulfilling and meaningful life. Supporting teenagers in this journey not only enhances their individual development but also contributes to the growth and well-being of our society as a whole.

ppp

*"Cultural and ethical values shape a teenager's worldview. Teach them the importance of respect, empathy, and responsibility. These values guide their actions and decisions."*

# EIGHTEEN

## COPING WITH FAILURE AND SETBACKS

Coping with failure and setbacks is a fundamental aspect of personal growth and resilience, especially during adolescence. Teenagers face numerous challenges as they navigate the complexities of growing up, and learning how to handle disappointments and failures is crucial for their development. Developing the ability to cope with setbacks involves fostering a growth mindset, building emotional resilience, and providing support and guidance to help teenagers learn from their experiences and move forward with confidence.

One of the most important aspects of coping with failure is understanding that it is a natural part of life. Everyone experiences setbacks at some point, and failure is not an indication of one's worth or potential. Helping teenagers reframe their perspective on failure is essential. Instead of viewing failure as a definitive end or a reflection of their abilities, they should see it as an opportunity for learning and growth. This shift in mindset can reduce the fear of failure and encourage a more positive and proactive approach to challenges.

A growth mindset, the belief that abilities and intelligence can be developed through effort and learning, is crucial for coping with failure. Encouraging teenagers to embrace this mindset involves emphasizing the value of effort, persistence, and learning from mistakes. Praising their hard work and resilience, rather than just their successes, can reinforce the idea that growth and improvement are possible through dedication and perseverance. By focusing on the process rather than the outcome, teenagers can develop a more resilient attitude toward failure and setbacks.

Building emotional resilience is another key component of coping with failure. Emotional resilience is the ability to adapt to stressful situations and bounce back from adversity. Developing resilience involves teaching teenagers how to manage their emotions, cope with stress, and maintain a positive outlook even in difficult times. Encouraging them to practice mindfulness, relaxation techniques, and positive self-talk can help them build emotional resilience. It is important to provide a supportive environment where they feel safe to express their emotions and discuss their experiences without fear of judgment or criticism.

Learning from failure is a critical part of the coping process. Encouraging teenagers to reflect on their setbacks and identify what went wrong and what they can do differently next time can help them gain valuable insights and improve their future performance. This process of self-reflection and analysis fosters a sense of agency and control, as they learn to view failure as a temporary setback rather than a permanent defeat. Providing constructive feedback and guidance can also help them identify areas for improvement and develop strategies for overcoming challenges.

Support and encouragement from parents, caregivers, and mentors are essential for helping teenagers cope with failure. Creating an environment of unconditional support and acceptance allows teenagers to feel safe and valued regardless of their successes or failures. Offering empathy and understanding, rather than criticism or disappointment, can help them feel more comfortable discussing their setbacks and seeking advice. Encouraging open communication and providing reassurance can boost their confidence and resilience. It is important to be patient and supportive, allowing them to navigate their own journey while offering guidance and encouragement along the way.

Encouraging teenagers to set realistic and achievable goals can also help them cope with failure. Setting overly ambitious or unrealistic goals can lead to frustration and disappointment, while setting attainable goals can provide a sense of accomplishment and motivation. Helping teenagers break down larger goals into smaller, manageable steps can make the process less overwhelming and more achievable. Celebrating their progress and achievements, no matter how small, can boost their confidence and reinforce their commitment to their goals.

Building a strong support network is crucial for coping with failure. Positive relationships with family, friends, teachers, and mentors provide a source of encouragement, guidance, and emotional support. Encouraging teenagers to seek out and maintain supportive relationships can help them feel connected and understood. These relationships can provide valuable perspectives, advice, and encouragement during difficult times. Participation in group activities, clubs, or support groups can also help them build a network of peers who share similar experiences and provide mutual support.

Developing problem-solving skills is another important aspect of coping with failure. Teaching teenagers how to approach problems methodically, consider different options, and evaluate potential solutions can empower them to tackle challenges more effectively. Encouraging them to think critically and creatively about solutions can help them develop a more proactive and resourceful approach to setbacks. Providing opportunities for them to practice problem-solving in various contexts can enhance their confidence and competence in handling challenges.

Encouraging self-compassion is essential for coping with failure. Teenagers can be their own harshest critics, and negative self-talk can exacerbate feelings of failure and inadequacy. Teaching them to practice self-compassion involves encouraging them to treat themselves with the same kindness and understanding they would offer a friend in a similar situation. Reminding them that everyone makes mistakes and experiences setbacks can help them develop a more forgiving and supportive attitude toward themselves. Encouraging them to focus on their strengths and accomplishments, rather than dwelling on their failures, can also boost their self-esteem and resilience.

Physical health and well-being play a significant role in coping with failure. Regular physical activity, a balanced diet, and adequate sleep are essential for maintaining energy levels, reducing stress, and enhancing overall well-being. Encouraging teenagers to prioritize self-care and engage in activities that promote physical and mental health can provide a solid foundation for resilience. Physical activity, in particular, has been shown to reduce symptoms of anxiety and depression, improve mood, and boost self-esteem. Encouraging them to find physical activities they enjoy can help them stay active and build resilience.

Cultural and societal influences can impact how teenagers perceive and cope with failure. Societal pressures to succeed and the stigma associated with failure can create additional stress and anxiety. It is important to challenge these cultural norms and promote a more balanced and realistic perspective on success and failure.

Encouraging teenagers to define success on their own terms and to focus on personal growth and fulfillment, rather than external validation, can help them develop a healthier attitude toward failure. Promoting a culture of learning, curiosity, and resilience, rather than one of perfectionism and competition, can create a more supportive environment for coping with setbacks.

Providing opportunities for personal growth and development can help teenagers build resilience and cope with failure. Encouraging them to pursue their interests, explore new activities, and take on challenges outside of their comfort zone can enhance their confidence and skills. Providing opportunities for leadership, creativity, and self-expression can help them develop a sense of purpose and fulfillment. Encouraging them to engage in community service or volunteer work can also provide a sense of accomplishment and connection to others.

Educating teenagers about the importance of perseverance and persistence is crucial for coping with failure. Success often requires sustained effort and the ability to keep going despite setbacks. Sharing stories of individuals who have overcome failures and achieved success through perseverance can provide inspiration and motivation. Encouraging teenagers to stay committed to their goals, even when faced with obstacles, can help them develop the determination and resilience needed to achieve their aspirations.

In conclusion, coping with failure and setbacks is a critical aspect of personal growth and resilience, especially during adolescence. By fostering a growth mindset, building emotional resilience, providing support and guidance, encouraging realistic goal-setting, developing problem-solving skills, promoting self-compassion, and prioritizing physical health and well-being, we can help teenagers navigate the challenges of failure and setbacks with confidence and resilience. Creating a supportive environment, challenging societal pressures, and providing opportunities for personal growth can empower teenagers to learn from their experiences and move forward with a positive and proactive attitude. Supporting teenagers in this journey not only enhances their current well-being but also prepares them for a lifetime of resilience, adaptability, and success.

ϷϷϷ

"Financial literacy is a crucial life skill. Educate teenagers about budgeting, saving, and responsible spending. This knowledge prepares them for financial independence."

# NINETEEN
## Encouraging Volunteerism and Empathy

Encouraging volunteerism and empathy in teenagers is vital for their development as compassionate, responsible, and engaged citizens. Volunteerism provides teenagers with the opportunity to contribute to their communities, develop valuable skills, and gain a sense of purpose and fulfillment. Empathy, the ability to understand and share the feelings of others, is fundamental for building strong, supportive relationships and fostering a more inclusive and caring society. By promoting volunteerism and empathy, we can help teenagers grow into adults who are not only successful but also kind, responsible, and community-minded.

Volunteerism offers numerous benefits for teenagers. It provides them with the chance to give back to their communities and make a positive impact on the lives of others. This sense of contribution and involvement can boost their self-esteem and provide a sense of accomplishment. Volunteering also helps teenagers develop important life skills, such as teamwork, communication, problem-solving, and leadership. These skills are valuable not only in their personal lives but also in their academic and professional careers. Additionally, volunteer work can expose teenagers to diverse perspectives and experiences, broadening their understanding of the world and fostering a sense of empathy and social responsibility.

Encouraging teenagers to volunteer can be done by providing opportunities and support. Schools, community organizations, and non-profits often have volunteer programs that welcome teenage involvement. Parents and caregivers can also play a role by helping teenagers find volunteer opportunities that align with their interests and passions. Whether it's working at a local food bank, participating in environmental clean-up efforts, or tutoring younger students, there are numerous ways for teenagers to get involved and make a difference. It is important to provide guidance and encouragement, helping them understand the value of their contributions and the impact they can have.

Empathy is closely linked to volunteerism, as both involve understanding and addressing the needs of others. Developing empathy in teenagers involves encouraging them to see the world from different perspectives and to appreciate the experiences and emotions of others. This can be fostered through open conversations about feelings, active listening, and exposure to diverse cultures and life experiences. Encouraging teenagers to read literature, watch films, and engage in discussions that explore different perspectives can enhance their ability to empathize with others. Practicing empathy in everyday interactions, such as being kind to peers, helping family members, and supporting friends, reinforces these values and helps teenagers build strong, supportive relationships.

One effective way to foster empathy and volunteerism is through experiential learning. Hands-on experiences, such as volunteering, community service projects, and service-learning programs, allow teenagers to engage directly with their communities and see the impact of their efforts. These experiences help them develop a deeper understanding of social issues and the challenges faced by others. By working alongside people from different backgrounds and circumstances, teenagers can develop empathy and a greater appreciation for diversity. Service-learning programs, which combine academic learning with community service, provide a structured way for teenagers to apply their knowledge and skills to real-world issues, further enhancing their empathy and social awareness.

Role modeling is another powerful way to encourage volunteerism and empathy in teenagers. Adults, including parents, teachers, and community leaders, can demonstrate these values through their own actions. When teenagers see adults actively involved in volunteer work and displaying empathy in their interactions, they are more likely to adopt these behaviors themselves. Sharing personal stories of volunteer experiences and discussing the importance of empathy in everyday life can also inspire teenagers to get involved and develop these qualities. Role models can provide guidance and support, helping teenagers navigate the challenges and rewards of volunteer work and empathetic behavior.

Creating a supportive environment that values and recognizes volunteerism and empathy is crucial. Schools and communities can celebrate and highlight the contributions of volunteers, providing recognition and appreciation for their efforts. Awards, certificates, and public acknowledgments can reinforce the importance of volunteer work and motivate teenagers to get involved. Encouraging peer support and collaboration in volunteer activities can also enhance the experience, making it more enjoyable and rewarding. By fostering a culture that values empathy and volunteerism, we can create an environment where these qualities are encouraged and celebrated.

Encouraging reflection is an important aspect of developing

empathy and a deeper understanding of volunteerism. After participating in volunteer activities, encouraging teenagers to reflect on their experiences can help them process what they have learned and how it has impacted them. Reflection can be done through discussions, journaling, or creative projects that allow teenagers to express their thoughts and feelings. Asking questions such as "What did you learn from this experience?" "How did it make you feel?" and "How did your actions impact others?" can help them gain insights and develop a more profound sense of empathy and social responsibility.

Education and awareness are also key components of fostering volunteerism and empathy. Providing teenagers with information about social issues, such as poverty, homelessness, environmental sustainability, and social justice, can help them understand the context and importance of their volunteer work. Educating them about the root causes of these issues and the ways in which they can contribute to solutions can empower them to take action. Schools and community organizations can offer workshops, seminars, and resources that provide this information and encourage critical thinking and informed action.

Encouraging teenagers to take initiative and develop their own volunteer projects can also be highly rewarding. By identifying a need in their community and creating a plan to address it, teenagers can develop leadership skills and a sense of ownership over their contributions. Providing support and guidance throughout the process can help them overcome challenges and achieve their goals. This sense of initiative and empowerment can foster a lifelong commitment to volunteerism and social responsibility.

Developing empathy also involves teaching teenagers about emotional intelligence. Emotional intelligence, the ability to recognize, understand, and manage one's own emotions and the emotions of others, is closely linked to empathy. Encouraging teenagers to practice self-awareness, self-regulation, and social skills can enhance their ability to empathize and connect with others. Activities such as mindfulness, role-playing, and conflict resolution exercises can help them develop these skills and improve their emotional intelligence.

Encouraging volunteerism and empathy also involves addressing barriers and challenges. Teenagers may face obstacles such as lack of time, transportation, or awareness of opportunities. Providing practical solutions, such as flexible volunteer schedules, transportation options, and accessible information about volunteer opportunities, can help them overcome these barriers. It is also important to address any misconceptions or fears they may have about volunteering or interacting with diverse populations. Providing reassurance, support, and positive experiences can help them feel more comfortable and confident in their volunteer work.

Engaging families in volunteer activities can also enhance the experience for teenagers. Family volunteer projects provide an opportunity for bonding, shared experiences, and mutual support. Families can work together on community service projects, participate in fundraising events, or support local non-profits. This collective effort can strengthen family relationships and create a sense of shared purpose and values. Encouraging families to discuss their volunteer experiences and the importance of empathy can reinforce these values and inspire continued involvement.

The long-term benefits of encouraging volunteerism and empathy in teenagers extend beyond individual development. By fostering these qualities, we contribute to the creation of a more compassionate, inclusive, and engaged society. Teenagers who develop a strong sense of empathy and a commitment to volunteerism are more likely to become adults who contribute positively to their communities and advocate for social justice and equity. They are better equipped to build meaningful relationships, understand diverse perspectives, and address complex social issues. Ultimately, encouraging volunteerism and empathy helps create a better world for everyone.

In conclusion, encouraging volunteerism and empathy in teenagers is essential for their development and the well-being of society. By providing opportunities, support, and guidance, we can help teenagers develop the skills, values, and attitudes needed to make a positive impact on their communities. Through volunteer work, experiential learning, role modeling, reflection, education, and family involvement, we can foster a sense of empathy and social responsibility in teenagers. Addressing barriers and challenges and creating a supportive environment that values and recognizes these qualities further enhances their development. By investing in the growth of empathetic and engaged teenagers, we contribute to a brighter and more compassionate future for all.

ᗺᗺᗺ

*"Balance is key in a teenager's life. Encourage a healthy mix of academic pursuits, physical activities, and social interactions. This balance supports holistic development."*

# TWENTY
## CREATING A SAFE AND SUPPORTIVE HOME ENVIRONMENT

Creating a safe and supportive home environment is fundamental to the healthy development and well-being of teenagers. This environment serves as the foundation where they can grow, learn, and thrive. It involves providing physical safety, emotional support, and fostering a sense of belonging and stability. As teenagers navigate the complexities of adolescence, a nurturing home environment can help them build resilience, develop healthy relationships, and achieve their full potential.

Physical safety is the first essential aspect of a supportive home environment. Ensuring that the home is free from hazards and risks is crucial. This includes taking steps to prevent accidents, securing dangerous items like medications and firearms, and maintaining a clean and organized living space. A safe home allows teenagers to move freely and confidently without fear of harm. Additionally, fostering an environment where rules and boundaries are clear and consistently enforced helps create a sense of security. Teenagers need to know what is expected of them and the consequences of their actions. This clarity helps them feel safe and understand the structure within which they operate.

Emotional support is equally important in creating a nurturing home environment. Adolescence is a time of emotional upheaval, as teenagers experience rapid changes in their bodies, emotions, and social relationships. Providing emotional support involves being present, listening actively, and validating their feelings. Parents and caregivers play a critical role in helping teenagers navigate their emotions by offering understanding, empathy, and guidance. Creating an open and non-judgmental atmosphere where teenagers feel comfortable expressing themselves is vital. Encouraging open communication and being approachable allows teenagers to share their concerns, fears, and joys without fear of criticism or rejection.

A sense of belonging and stability is crucial for teenagers' development. They need to feel that they are an integral part of the family and that their contributions are valued. This involves fostering a sense of connection and togetherness through family activities, traditions, and rituals. Spending quality time together, whether through shared meals, outings, or family projects, helps strengthen family bonds and creates lasting memories. Stability also means providing a consistent and predictable environment. While flexibility is important, maintaining routines and traditions provides a sense of normalcy and security. Teenagers need to know that they can rely on their home as a stable and dependable place.

Promoting positive relationships within the home is essential for creating a supportive environment. Healthy relationships with parents, siblings, and other family members provide a foundation of trust and mutual respect. Encouraging positive interactions, effective communication, and conflict resolution skills helps build strong and supportive relationships. It is important to model these behaviors as parents and caregivers, demonstrating how to navigate conflicts constructively and communicate openly and respectfully. Building positive relationships also involves recognizing and celebrating each family member's individuality and contributions. Acknowledging achievements, providing encouragement, and showing appreciation fosters a positive and supportive atmosphere.

Supporting teenagers' autonomy and independence is a key aspect of a supportive home environment. As they grow, teenagers need opportunities to make decisions, take on responsibilities, and learn from their experiences. Encouraging autonomy involves trusting them to make choices and supporting them in taking on new challenges. This helps them develop confidence and a sense of responsibility. Providing opportunities for teenagers to contribute to household tasks, manage their own schedules, and make decisions about their activities fosters independence. It is important to strike a balance between providing guidance and allowing them the freedom to learn and grow on their own.

Educational support is another critical component of a supportive home environment. Encouraging academic achievement and a love of learning helps teenagers reach their full potential. This involves creating a conducive study environment, providing access to educational resources, and supporting their academic endeavors. Showing interest in their schoolwork, attending parent-teacher conferences, and celebrating their achievements reinforces the importance of education. It is also important to provide support and guidance when they face academic challenges, helping them develop effective study habits, problem-solving skills, and resilience.

Supporting teenagers' social development is crucial for their overall well-being. Encouraging positive peer relationships and providing opportunities for social interaction helps them build social skills and a sense of belonging. This can involve facilitating their involvement in extracurricular activities, sports, clubs, and community events. Providing guidance on navigating social dynamics, such as dealing with peer pressure and resolving conflicts, helps them develop healthy and positive relationships. It is also important to be aware of their social interactions and provide support and intervention when necessary to ensure their safety and well-being.

Fostering a positive and healthy lifestyle is essential for teenagers' development. Encouraging regular physical activity, a balanced diet, and adequate sleep supports their physical health and well-being. Providing nutritious meals, promoting regular exercise, and establishing healthy sleep routines helps teenagers maintain their energy levels and overall health. Encouraging healthy habits, such as limiting screen time and promoting outdoor activities, supports their physical and mental well-being. It is important to model these healthy behaviors as parents and caregivers, demonstrating the importance of self-care and a balanced lifestyle.

Mental health support is a crucial aspect of a supportive home environment. Adolescence can be a challenging time, with teenagers experiencing stress, anxiety, and other mental health issues. Providing mental health support involves being attentive to their emotional well-being, recognizing signs of distress, and offering appropriate support and intervention. Encouraging open conversations about mental health, reducing stigma, and promoting coping strategies helps teenagers manage their emotions and seek help when needed. Providing access to mental health resources, such as counseling and therapy, supports their mental health and well-being. It is important to create an environment where teenagers feel comfortable seeking help and discussing their mental health concerns.

Encouraging self-expression and creativity is important for teenagers' development. Providing opportunities for them to explore their interests, talents, and passions helps them develop a sense of identity and self-worth. This can involve supporting their involvement in arts, music, sports, and other creative activities. Encouraging them to express themselves through writing, drawing, or other creative outlets fosters a sense of individuality and self-confidence. It is important to provide a supportive and non-judgmental environment where they feel free to explore and express their creativity.

Cultural and ethical values play a significant role in creating a supportive home environment. Teaching teenagers about the importance of values such as respect, empathy, honesty, and responsibility helps them develop a strong moral foundation. Encouraging them to understand and appreciate their cultural heritage fosters a sense of identity and pride. Providing opportunities for them to engage in cultural activities and traditions helps them stay connected to their roots. It is also important to encourage them to respect and appreciate diversity, fostering an inclusive and empathetic outlook.

Financial literacy is an important aspect of preparing teenagers for the future. Teaching them about money management, budgeting, saving, and financial planning helps them develop responsible financial habits. Providing opportunities for them to manage their own money, whether through an allowance or part-time job, helps them develop practical financial skills. Encouraging discussions about financial goals and responsibilities helps them understand the importance of financial planning and stability.

Technology and media literacy are crucial in today's digital age. Teaching teenagers about responsible and safe use of technology, internet safety, and digital citizenship helps them navigate the digital world effectively. Encouraging them to critically evaluate the information they encounter online and to be mindful of their digital footprint promotes responsible technology use. Providing guidance on balancing screen time with other activities supports their overall well-being. It is important to model responsible technology use and to establish guidelines and boundaries for technology use within the home.

Building resilience and coping skills is essential for teenagers' development. Teaching them how to manage stress, handle setbacks, and bounce back from challenges helps them develop resilience. Encouraging them to develop healthy coping strategies, such as mindfulness, exercise, and seeking support, helps them navigate difficult times. Providing a supportive environment where they feel safe to take risks and learn from their experiences fosters resilience. It is important to provide encouragement and support, helping them develop a positive and proactive approach to challenges.

In conclusion, creating a safe and supportive home environment involves providing physical safety, emotional support, a sense of belonging, and stability. It involves fostering positive relationships, supporting autonomy and independence, encouraging educational and social development, promoting a healthy lifestyle, and providing mental health support. It also involves encouraging self-expression, teaching cultural and ethical values, promoting financial literacy, and guiding responsible technology use. By providing a nurturing and supportive environment, parents and caregivers can help teenagers develop the skills, confidence, and resilience needed to navigate the challenges of adolescence and achieve their full potential. Supporting teenagers in this journey not only enhances their individual well-being but also contributes to the growth and well-being of the family and community as a whole.

ᑭᑭᑭ

"*Fostering a growth mindset empowers teenagers to embrace challenges. Encourage them to view effort as a path to mastery. This mindset builds resilience and a love of learning.*"

# TWENTY-ONE
## SUMMARY

In the contemporary world, technology permeates nearly every aspect of our lives, particularly in the realm of education. Digital learning has transformed traditional educational models, offering unprecedented access to information and resources. However, the rapid integration of technology into learning environments also presents ethical challenges that must be addressed to ensure that digital education is conducted responsibly and equitably. "Tech with Heart: Integrating Ethics into Digital Learning" emphasizes the need to weave ethical considerations into the fabric of digital education. This approach ensures that technological advancements enhance learning experiences without compromising values such as privacy, equity, and inclusivity.

The foundation of ethical digital learning begins with understanding and respecting privacy. In an age where data is a valuable commodity, the protection of students' personal information is paramount. Educational institutions and technology providers must implement robust data security measures to safeguard sensitive information. This involves using encryption, secure storage solutions, and regular audits to prevent unauthorized access and breaches. Additionally, students and their families should be educated about data privacy, helping them understand what data is being collected, how it is used, and their rights regarding this information. Transparent policies and practices build trust and foster a safer digital learning environment.

Equity is another critical pillar of ethical digital learning. While technology has the potential to bridge educational gaps, it can also exacerbate inequalities if not carefully managed. Access to digital tools and the internet varies widely among students, influenced by socio-economic status, geographic location, and other factors. To ensure that all students benefit from digital learning, efforts must be made to provide equitable access to technology. This can include initiatives such as providing devices to students who lack them, ensuring reliable internet access, and offering training for both students and educators on how to effectively use digital tools. Moreover, digital content should be designed to be accessible to all learners, including those with disabilities. This involves following accessibility guidelines, such as providing screen reader-compatible content and ensuring that multimedia resources include captions and transcripts.

Inclusivity in digital learning goes beyond access to technology; it encompasses the creation of a supportive and engaging learning environment for all students. This means designing curricula and resources that reflect diverse perspectives and cultures, promoting a sense of belonging and respect among students. Educators should be trained to recognize and counteract biases, both in their teaching and in the digital tools they use. Inclusive practices also involve encouraging student participation and voice in their learning experiences, allowing them to share their unique perspectives and contribute to the learning community.

The ethical use of artificial intelligence (AI) and machine learning in education is a growing concern. These technologies hold great promise for personalized learning and administrative efficiencies, but they also raise ethical questions about bias, transparency, and accountability. AI systems can inadvertently perpetuate biases present in their training data, leading to unfair or discriminatory outcomes. To mitigate these risks, it is essential to implement rigorous testing and validation processes to ensure that AI systems are fair and unbiased. Transparency in how AI-driven decisions are made and providing explanations for these decisions are crucial for maintaining trust. Additionally, there should be clear accountability mechanisms in place, ensuring that there are avenues for addressing grievances and rectifying any harms caused by AI systems.

Digital literacy is an essential component of ethical digital learning. Students must be equipped with the skills to navigate the digital world safely and responsibly. This includes understanding how to evaluate the credibility of online information, recognizing and avoiding cyber threats, and maintaining a healthy digital footprint. Digital literacy education should also cover the ethical implications of technology use, such as the importance of respecting intellectual property, understanding the impact of online behavior, and being aware of digital etiquette. By fostering digital literacy, we empower students to become responsible digital citizens who can critically engage with technology and its societal impacts.

Educators play a pivotal role in integrating ethics into digital learning. They must model ethical behavior and guide students in navigating the ethical dilemmas that arise in digital environments. Professional development and ongoing training for educators are essential to ensure they are equipped with the knowledge and skills to address these challenges. This includes training on data privacy, digital equity, inclusive teaching practices, and the ethical use of technology. Educators should also be encouraged to foster an open dialogue about ethics in their classrooms, creating a space where students can explore and discuss ethical issues related to digital learning.

Parental involvement is another crucial aspect of ethical digital learning. Parents and guardians should be engaged in conversations about their children's digital education and the ethical considerations it entails. Schools and educators can support this by providing resources and guidance on how to promote safe and responsible technology use at home. This partnership between educators and families helps reinforce ethical practices and ensures a consistent approach to digital learning.

The role of policy and regulation in promoting ethical digital learning cannot be overstated. Governments and educational authorities must establish clear guidelines and standards for the ethical use of technology in education. This includes setting standards for data privacy, ensuring equitable access to digital resources, and promoting inclusive practices. Regulatory frameworks should also address the ethical use of AI and other emerging technologies in education, providing oversight and accountability mechanisms. Collaboration between policymakers, educators, technology providers, and other stakeholders is essential to develop and implement these guidelines effectively.

Ethical digital learning also involves fostering a culture of continuous reflection and improvement. As technology evolves, so too do the ethical challenges it presents. Educational institutions and technology providers must remain vigilant and proactive in addressing these issues. This involves regularly reviewing and updating policies and practices, staying informed about emerging ethical concerns, and seeking feedback from students, educators, and other stakeholders. By adopting a proactive and reflective approach, we can ensure that digital learning continues to evolve in a way that aligns with ethical values and principles.

The global nature of digital learning further underscores the importance of ethics. Digital education transcends geographical boundaries, connecting learners and educators from diverse cultural and socio-economic backgrounds. This interconnectedness requires a commitment to global ethical standards that respect cultural differences while promoting fundamental values such as equity, inclusivity, and respect for human rights. International collaboration and dialogue are essential for developing and maintaining these standards, ensuring that digital learning benefits all learners regardless of their location.

Finally, ethical digital learning involves preparing students for the ethical challenges they will face in the broader digital world. This preparation extends beyond the classroom, equipping students with the tools and mindset to navigate ethical dilemmas in their personal and professional lives. By integrating ethics into digital learning, we help students develop a strong moral compass and the critical thinking skills needed to make informed and ethical decisions in an increasingly complex and digital world.

In summary, "Tech with Heart: Integrating Ethics into Digital Learning" emphasizes the importance of embedding ethical considerations into every aspect of digital education. This approach ensures that technological advancements enhance learning experiences without compromising values such as privacy, equity, inclusivity, and integrity. By fostering a culture of ethical awareness and responsibility, we can create a digital learning environment that not only prepares students for academic and professional success but also cultivates compassionate, responsible, and engaged citizens. Through collaboration, education, and a commitment to continuous improvement, we can navigate the ethical challenges of digital learning and harness the full potential of technology to create a better and more just world for all learners.

ᑭᑭᑭ

# Citation And References

This book represents the culmination of extensive research and meticulous analysis, incorporating a diverse range of sources, including numerous books, scholarly studies, and personal experiences. Additionally, I have scoured various websites to gather relevant information and data essential for the compilation of this work. I have taken every precaution to ensure the accuracy of the information presented and have diligently cited all sources to acknowledge their contributions.

Despite these efforts, the possibility of inadvertent errors remains. I deeply value the insights of my readers and appreciate any feedback that can help identify and rectify such inaccuracies. I encourage you to bring any discrepancies to my attention.

Your feedback is not only welcome but crucial, as it will aid in correcting current editions and enhancing the content of future ones. I am committed to maintaining the highest standards of accuracy and reliability in my work and thank you for your support and understanding.

Additionally, I firmly uphold the principle of freedom of speech and expression as guaranteed under Article 19(1)(a) of the Constitution of India, and I respect the diverse viewpoints and expressions of all readers.

ᠵᠵᠵ

# Other Books Of The Author

1. Empowering Minds: A Journey into Women's Self-Discovery and Power
2. The Dynamics of Motivation: Catalyzing Thought into Action
3. Meditation and Mental Well Being: The Path to Inner Peace and Clarity
4. The Psychology of Child Education: Nurturing Future Generations
5. Ethical Enlightenment: A Modern Guide to Living with Integrity
6. Voices of Empowerment: Stories of Women Rising Against Odds
7. Social Psychology in Everyday Life: Understanding Human Connections
8. The Essence of Motivational Speaking: Inspiring Change in Others
9. Balancing Acts: Women, Work, and the Will to Lead
10. Guiding with Grace: Raising Children with Compassion and Awareness
11. The Power of Positive Aging: Embracing Life After Fifty
12. Building Resilient Communities: Social Work in Action
13. The Ethical Educator: Principles for Teaching and Learning
14. From Insight to Impact: Social Psychology for a Better World
15. The Ethics of Empathy: A Guide to Ethical Living
16. The Science of Empowering the Self: Navigating Life's Challenges with Psychological Wisdom
17. The Mindful Conscious Leader: Meditation Techniques for Modern Management
18. Pioneering Spirit: Women's Pathways to Leadership and Empowerment
19. Feeling to Healing: The Role of Emotional Intelligence in Child Development
20. Transformative Talks and Words of Inspiration: Insights into Motivational Oratory

Bhajan
101.   Pilgrimage of the Soul: Spiritual Journeys in India

❧❧❧

# Contact

Dr. Minakshi Bansal
Social Activist
Ahmedabad, Gujarat, Bharat
minakshiindiag20@yahoo.com

ΡΡΡ

**|| LOKAHA SAMASTHAHA SUKHINO BHAVANTU ||**

9 798894 469041